If you need immedia  **1eck**
out the last page o   **rst**
steps that you can ~~take~~ ...   ;.

There are also suggestions at the end of each chapter
that may be relevant to you.
You can reflect upon your own progress
and that of the person within the story.

For the general reader

This book is not just for the anxious.
It is a story of a woman struggling to overcome past experiences.
There are aspects of all of us within this story.

There
& back again

RECOVERY FROM
ANXIETY
AND SO MUCH MORE

AMANDA MCKEE

STONE'S THROW
PUBLICATIONS

Editing, cover and interior design: Sue Reynolds,
Piquant Productions

Cover photo: bigstockphoto.com/Paolo Gallo
Back Cover Author Photo: Des McKee

Published by **Stones Throw Publications**
13240 Mast Rd., Port Perry, ON L9L 1B5

ISBN: 978-1-987813-59-3 pbk

Printed and bound in Canada

1 2 3 4 5 6 7 8 9 10

*He was an Englishman, which is to say that
the language of emotion was not his first language.
Rather it was like Latin, or French,
someone could study and understand
but never fully master.*

~ Malcolm Gladwell

Introduction

On a bright, crisp, incredibly cold Canadian winter's day I was sitting in the warmth of a restaurant with a group of volunteers. As I chatted with the organizer, she told me she was worried about her sister who'd just turned fifty and was suffering from anxiety. My reaction was a soothing statement. "That's quite common when women hit menopause." But behind my calm statement was a lot of churning emotion. There was so much more to say. I knew firsthand how debilitating anxiety could be but I wasn't about to admit to my struggle with mental illness at this pleasant lunch. I made some vague suggestions about drugs and therapy, but as we talked I became more engaged. I could so identify with her sister and this anxiety. I quietly told her that I had suffered from anxiety when I turned fifty. She was interested and wanted to know how I'd dealt with it. How had I recovered? She wanted answers for her sister. I remembered what it was like to want those answers. I remembered wanting desperately to know how to get well.

I took a deep breath, hesitated while I was searching for a simple answer, then said, "I wish I'd taken the medication earlier. I truly think this would have helped me." But I knew this was far from a complete answer. It's complex. Each person is an individual and their anxiety can have multiple causes. I wished that I'd known what I know now when I'd been dealing with anxiety.

The organizer suggested I should write about my experiences. Later, I became distracted by the idea that I could put my story to paper, although it was a story much greater that just anxiety. I didn't know how to do this, how to start. It was difficult to sift through my perceptions, past and present, to find the true reality. But perhaps, there was no truth, just my shifting perspectives? I'd become a different person who understood my world differently. Perhaps my experiences could help someone else who was struggling with anxiety. Out of all these thoughts, the following story of Julia was born.

1954

A little girl sits quietly on an outdoor bench swinging her legs—legs that nowhere near touch the ground. It's cold and grey. The ground is wet although it's not raining now. She's bundled up in a wool coat. Beside her sits her father his head dropped forward. He's asleep. He has been for a while. She's got to stay here quietly so that when he wakes up they can continue exploring the little zoo. But when he does wake, it's too late, they need to go. He has to get back to work.

Chapter 1

Anxiety and Sleeping—how did she get there?

Julia sits waiting outside the therapist's office, outwardly calm, but inside feeling tension. She doesn't know what to expect from this appointment, she's never been to therapy. She hopes that the solutions to her problems lie behind those tall doors. The quiet surroundings are suddenly punctuated by a click as one of those doors opens. A man walks past her without looking right or left and disappears through the exit.

A pretty young women appears at the door. "Please come in. It's Julia, isn't it? I'm Karen."

Julia feels her heart beating as she follows the therapist into the large airy room.

"Please take a seat," says Karen, indicating a group of four, old style, comfortable-looking arm chairs.

Julia chooses the one facing the window. Karen takes a folder from her desk and then sits in the seat opposite Julia. A quiet, calm air of confidence emanates from her as she settles in.

Julia sits up but back in the chair, hoping to make a good impression.

Karen starts the session by saying, "What brings you here today?"

"I'm not sleeping well and then I get anxious. I know things need to change. I thought a few therapy sessions would help me sort out the problem." What Julia doesn't say is, *The anxiety is so awful, at times, it consumes my whole existence.*

Julia's mind flips back to that January night a few weeks ago. At about 2:00 am she'd been sitting at the kitchen table, shaking. Her husband, Len, held her hands. She was in a desperate place: her world was tumbling down. She'd told Len, "This anxiety is terrible, I'm exhausted, I need to sleep or I can't work, I'm just completely lost. I really want to keep working because I enjoy it. It gives me my identity."

Len nodded. "Perhaps you can go back to work part time? Maybe that could relieve some of the pressure."

With his suggestion, Julia could feel some of the tension flow out of her, "And perhaps I could go to those free therapy sessions that are offered through my employer?" These ideas allowed her to feel some measure of control which felt so much better.

So here she is at Karen's office, hoping that she is doing the right thing for herself, hoping that the therapy will solve her sleeping problem.

Karen's voice is gentle and kind. "So, let's start with your work. Tell me about it."

Julia relaxes a little into her chair. "Well, I'm a secondary school teacher. I enjoy the work of teaching and interacting with the students. But these days, there's so much more paper work tracking and recording the progress of the kids. That's on top of writing new course material and experimenting with new methods of teaching. And the students are challenging authority more. The work never seems to end. I also have two teenage kids of my own. That's why I decided to go part time this semester. It helps, but I still struggle with sleep and get anxious about not sleeping. I've seen the doctor about this and have some sleeping pills but I don't like to take them too often."

Karen slowly nods and writes some notes into the folder on her lap. "You seem to be doing the right things to help yourself."

"I'm trying, but I'm still very anxious about sleeping. I thought going part time would relieve it. But it hasn't."

"It may take time for your anxiety to go away. As you feel more comfortable with the situation it should get less. What about your colleagues. Do you find that they are supportive?"

"Yes. Many of them are great. But there are some that I just don't understand. They say or do things and then I'm upset for days."

"Like what for instance?"

Julia shrugs her shoulders. "Some just don't seem to care about the kids. Others just don't seem to want to do their fair share of work."

"And does your family add to your stress?"

Julia pauses before she answers, "My husband is very support-ive and the kids are doing well at school. But yes, it is tiring keeping track of everything."

"What about your family of origin? I can tell from your accent that you're from Britain."

Julia feels a resistance. *What does this have to do with me not sleeping?* "Oh I think I was lonely as a child. We lived out in the country in a large house. Not many friends around. I spent a lot of time playing on my own outside in the garden. My two older sisters were always out horseback riding. I would have loved to have gone with them but I wasn't allowed." Julia starts to choke up a little. "My Dad was rarely home. He worked long hours in his own business. Mum was busy too, because we also had four lodgers living in the house as well as my grandparents. Grandma was an invalid on canes and Grandpa was gruff and distant. He often said 'Children should be seen and not heard.' Sometimes I was frightened that there were ghosts in that house. It was at least four hundred years old with lots of dark nooks and crannies."

Karen and Julia talk for almost an hour, Karen making notes as they talk. At the end, she looked up. "Your distress is so clear. It's also obvious that you are struggling to meet all of the demands placed on you by both your job and yourself. You are worrying a lot and have difficulty dealing with people." Karen looks down at her notes and then back up at Julia, "I think you would benefit from keeping a journal. It will give you an outlet for your anxiety. And, I think that we need to meet for several more sessions."

Julia is immediately suspicious. *Is Karen trying to extend the therapy unnecessarily? But still, my employer will cover two more sessions, what's the harm in making two more appointments?*

During the drive home, Julia feels very tired and a little disappointed. She'd expected Karen to say, "Okay you need to do this, this and this, then you'll start sleeping again." But that hadn't happened.

Maybe there isn't going to be a simple solution. Is this therapy going to work and be worth the time? Even so, she thinks, *I'm going to start a journal and see where it goes.*

Journal

What did I learn?

1. Keep a journal.
2. Live in the present. Worrying about the future uses up energy unproductively.
3. Address problems with people otherwise there is a lot of stored emotion, anger and loss of energy. If the problem cannot be addressed let it go.
4. Give yourself a break. Stop working so hard. Your lack of sleep is your body's way of making you take time for yourself. When you don't sleep you become so tired that you have to stop.

Julia rereads her basic journal entry and feels a wave of elation. Karen has given her a set of instructions to get better. *Now all I have to do is adopt these changes, then I'll feel relaxed and have more energy for living. I'll be less tired and I won't get anxious about the sleeping. I'm not really sure why she wanted me to start a journal but I've done that. It was easy. So now, how to address worrying about the future?*

She buys a little book with a cover that says, *Don't sweat the small stuff and It's all small stuff* by Richard Carlson. One afternoon, as she's reading snippets from the book, she shifts in her seat. *Yes, I do get caught up in thinking and thinking about things to come, but I'm just trying to work out what's best for me. I feel more relaxed if I have a plan, It's just the way I am. It's really difficult not to worry about the future.*

Meanwhile, she can feel anxiety rising within her about sleep that night. *How do I turn this off and stop it from overwhelming me?* That night she takes a sleeping pill.

The next day Julia feels exhausted by the end of her morning teaching but she stays into the afternoon to get the photocopying done for the following day.

Christine comes in. "I've only got one copy here. Can I just slip in?"

"Yes, of course." Julia moves out of the way.

But Christine doesn't have one copy to do, she has a class set of thirty.

Julia's annoyed. *This is my time she's wasting. Time when I should have been home. She takes a deep breath. This is my chance, she thinks, I can address this problem with Christine instead of keeping my feelings in and 'wasting energy'.*

"That's not just one copy."

As the photocopier throws out Christine's last page, she looks at Julia with disdain. "You're so unreasonable." And then, thirty copies in hand, she's gone, holding her head high.

Julia's heart is pounding. She feels exhausted and fearful. *This doesn't feel better than my original annoyance!* For the rest of the afternoon, she keeps thinking of how she could have responded differently. This fleeting confrontation has left her drained.

As the week goes on, Julia thinks about Karen's statement, 'Your lack of sleep is your body's way of making you take time for yourself.' The scientific part of her mind thinks, *That is a fascinating concept. Am I actually causing my own sleeplessness by ignoring my needs and doing too much?*

She thinks about how her life is filled with things that she feels she *has* to do, such as planning her lessons carefully, looking after her own kids and doing things at home. She always does too much.

But I've changed my work to part time, I am cutting back. Even so, she can feel a niggle in the back of her mind. Her afternoons are full of activities. She's listening to self-help CD's, doing workbooks and reading books on anxiety. She's devoting so much more time to the house, the garden and the kids. *I'm at work less, but I haven't really cut back.*

She sighs. *Why is all this so difficult?*

At the end of the week Julia goes to her second appointment with Karen. This time she doesn't feel so uptight as she waits.

When the door clicks open Karen is standing there. "Come on in."

Julia chooses the same seat as before.

Karen sits opposite her. "How have you been?"

Julia gives a deep sigh. "I'm not sleeping any better and changes aren't coming easily. I tried to do less this week but there are so many things that need to be done. And that thing of addressing problems with people just leads to confrontation."

"What happened?" Karen listens to Julia's story about the photocopying and then quietly looks at her. "You know it takes practice dealing with other people. Perhaps you could try saying 'I feel upset by...whatever it is...instead of telling the other person that their actions are unreasonable. It takes time to find your authentic voice, to find what works for you. It's worth persisting at this, but try to feel relaxed about it."

11

Julia nods.

Karen, then settles back into her chair. "So tell me, what did you do for fun this week?"

Julia looks perplexed. "Well—" She hesitates. "I was able to go to my son's indoor soccer game without feeling exhausted."

Karen tips her head a little to one side and studies her. "Do you think you have a balanced life between work and relaxation Julia?"

"I do spend a lot of time resting and reading about anxiety and sleep."

Karen opens the folder on her lap and jots down a note. "Yes, that is time for you. But are there any activities that you enjoy doing?"

"I'm busy. But we do have fun going for walks on the weekend with the kids, although it's a bit cold this time of year."

"It sounds to me as if you leave little time for yourself and that can be exhausting. It will really help, if you can find time for an activity that you enjoy. Think of this as homework until our next session. We can talk more then. Now I would like to look a little more deeply into your past. I think it could be valuable." Karen's voice is empathetic and caring. "Tell me more about your family in Britain."

Suddenly Julia is close to tears. *This is so difficult,* she thinks. Without thinking, she takes a leap and trusts Karen. "I was frightened of my father."

Karen sits up a little straighter. "Can you tell me about this?"

"He had a temper," says Julia, "and I never knew if I'd done something wrong. He would hit out if he was upset, it frightened and hurt me."

"Did this happen often?"

"No, he was away a lot working, I guess I was lucky." Julia chokes back tears.

1958

She's cleaning the inside of her dad's car, her Sunday afternoon chore each week. There's lots of dusting and polishing to do. The car is parked in the backyard below the house, away from anyone. Her sisters are off horse-back riding, as they do most Sundays. She turns the radio on so she won't mind being on her own. Then she sees her father coming towards the car. He seems upset. She tenses up. *What have I done wrong?* He opens the car door, leans in and snaps off the radio. He shouts at her to do the cleaning properly. Then he slams the door and he's gone. She relaxes a little, although her heart is beating very fast. But she's grateful. She got off lightly this time.

Journal, cont'd

Karen told me:

1. You hold in your emotions and don't let them go. This takes up a lot of energy, this partly explains your fatigue.
2. You don't have a balanced life between work and play.
3. You have a great deal of sadness about your childhood. This is affecting your life now, affecting your anxiety.

Today I told her that I'd been physically abused as a child. I've only ever talked about this once before when my children were little. I told my eldest sister that I would never hit my kids because of Dad. She blanched but said nothing and the subject was dropped. I had the feeling that she too had buried this aspect of her life and wasn't willing to talk about this painful part of our upbringing now.

Telling Karen was complicated, difficult and painful. I felt ashamed that I was betraying a trust and that I was over-dramatizing my situation. I couldn't talk about it without crying and crying. This was a very important session for me. Maybe there's truth to the idea that suppressed emotions cause exhaustion. I've been carrying all this buried baggage around for so long—such a weight dragging me down.

I'm beginning to get it. Maybe this problem of mine is deeper than not being able to sleep. Whenever I talk and write about my childhood, I feel overwhelmed by sadness. I can't help crying. The time has come for me to deal with these past secrets and free myself.

Near the end of February, Julia is again sitting outside Karen's office, this time waiting for her last visit. She enters the office feeling so much more relaxed and sits in her usual chair. But as she talks more about her past she begins to cry again. Karen quietly pushes the box of tissues over towards her.

Julia doesn't yet understand all the long-term effects that her upbringing has had on her. Her buried childhood memories are holding her in a place that creates unrelenting tension, tying her down to a difficult inner world. Her perception of the whole world is pushed through these background filters, colouring and affecting her life. But she's not aware of this. Now at last, with the therapy that Karen offers, Julia has a chance to break free from these forces.

Just before the end of the session Karen gently says, "I know this is your last session of therapy covered by your employer, but I encourage you to think about more sessions for which you will have to pay. You can choose how frequently we meet. It could be once a month."

Ever careful about money, Julia thinks, *We could afford once a month, I like Karen she gives me good advice.* Gone is the suspicion of Karen that she had felt after the first session. "Okay I'll make an appointment for the end of next month."

My crying doesn't seem to stop. Karen says these are tears that were never shed, that I'm grieving for the past. She has encouraged me to revisit those incidents, allow myself to feel the suppressed emotions and journal. I feel very pathetic. To add to that, I feel like I'm not getting better. I'm afraid I'll never sleep properly again—maybe that I'll never be well again. My heart beats fast, my neck and shoulders ache, I'm hot and I can't concentrate and settle to anything. I'm very distracted and generally feel terrible. I have no appetite.

Going through my mind is this continuous fear of not sleeping. How am I going to cope? How am I going to go to work (even though I'm only working part time now)? I feel at my wits' end. I try to think positive thoughts and try to tell myself that things will be okay, but the anxiety doesn't abate. I don't want to take drugs—I'm afraid of becoming dependent on them.

March 2 1998

I'm experimenting with alternative remedies—passion flower, valerian and melatonin—but nothing seems to help me sleep. I feel overwhelmed. It's only afternoon and I'm already becoming anxious about not sleeping tonight. I feel so fearful! I pace about, I get hot and cold, I can't concentrate on things. I keep obsessing about how bad I feel.

I can see why people turn to drugs or alcohol. I've been thinking about all my options: which doctors I should see. Maybe a naturopath? What about a hypnotist? Surely <u>they</u> can get me to sleep!

I've checked into lots of antidepressants but they have so many side effects and I don't want to become addicted to them.

I wish the anxiety wasn't so easily triggered. The thought that these destructive emotions can quickly appear again causes me more anxiety. No wonder I'm spinning round trying to find something that will give relief.

March 13, 1998

I tried very hard to sleep naturally last night. Tried a hot bath and deep relaxing breathing but I ended up taking a sleeping pill. I feel like such a failure. Why is this so elusive? Even little children can sleep.

March 15 1998

I need to go over to my family in England. My Dad is beginning to show signs of dementia and as a family, we have some legal things that have to be sorted out. The timing is not right for me. I really don't want to go. I can feel an anxiety growing inside me, mainly about not sleeping. This will be a very difficult journey.

March 28, 1998

By the time I was waiting at the airport I was beginning to shake because I was so anxious about sleep. The relaxation disc that I was listening to didn't calm me down—in fact it made it worse. I had to turn it off. I felt so hot, frightened and uncomfortable, I began to pace about. It wasn't that I felt anxious about the flight; that was easy, I just felt anxious about being in England. But once I got on the plane I calmed down. I'd flown lots of times on my own before and it felt familiar to me.

Thankfully the trip turned out okay. I passed my tiredness off as jet lag and used some sleeping pills. With the help of Mum's solicitor, we completed the legal matters, so in that respect the trip was successful. But my perception about my family shifted a little while I was there. I'd always felt that Dad was the problem in my life. He was never there for us children. And then his temper! He would snap so quickly. I remember the fear that I felt when I was around him.

But had Mum played a role in my insecurities as well? When I saw her with Dad, I realized this was absolutely the case. She was negating his feelings, belittling him, trying to bring him round to her point of view, just like she did with me when I was younger. I remember her telling me, "Of course you don't like horseback riding" when that was exactly what I wanted to do. The more I think about it, the more I realize that she was the one that I relied on but she always contradicted any feelings I tried to express. So my feelings were never validated, always undercut and denied. If I said I was upset she told me I didn't feel that way, and then convinced me I should be ashamed of myself for saying I felt that way.

I understand now, it was her way of trying to protect me from being hurt, but it didn't work. Now here I am, as an adult, distrustful of the whole world and feeling that I'm doing everything wrong. Confidence in my own judgment is elusive, I'm walking on eggshells all the time. I have difficulty getting close to anyone and I'm always seeking approval, especially from authority figures.

I just seem to be a bundle of insecurities. I guess deep down I've always known something was wrong but I wouldn't admit it. I adopted the idea that I had to deny my own feelings and push them aside. It makes me feel angry and helpless to realize what a huge toll this has taken from me over the years.

1958

It's a cold dark rainy day. She's walking up the steep hill of the lane to her home. This country lane is so old that it has been worn down below the level of the surrounding fields. She's on a relatively level part when it begins to rain. It really rains. She's absolutely soaked, buffeted by the strong wind, cold and exhausted. She's nearing the one cottage before her house. It's the home of her family's housekeeper. She needs to shelter until the rain ceases so she very tentatively knocks on the back door—she's been told "You mustn't intrude upon other people."

But she doesn't seem to be an intrusion. She's welcomed and she receives a great deal of sympathy and attention. It feels so good to be so cared for, especially since she was scared she was doing the wrong thing. The housekeeper and her family reassure her that she's welcome any time. She feels so comforted. But the next day her mother pulls her aside, tells her, "You must not intrude on other people! What on earth will they think of you?!"

She feels ashamed, she did the wrong thing. The family down the lane didn't want her there after all. Her instincts told her she was welcome but now she's told she was very wrong. She's very confused. Perhaps those instincts need to be buried. They only ever lead her into trouble.

April 2 1998

I woke up this morning feeling that I have no identity. That's what my tears are about. I'm not depressed I'm just shedding tears for the past. I never really considered how sad all this is for me.

I asked Karen "When will this sadness go away?"

She replied, "How long do you think it takes to recover from the loss of a child?"

That took me aback. I never thought of it this way: what I'd lost, the pain it caused and how difficult it is to get past it all. As I think more and more about me, I get flashes of insight. How I've always kept myself exhaustively busy so that I don't have to deal with my problems. It's time for me to reflect and grieve those things that caused me to withdraw into myself.

I can't deny that part of all this is the Catholic school upbringing, the rigidness and fear that the nuns instilled in me. You must always do the right thing no matter the cost; you must always put others before yourself; God will punish you if you don't 'behave'. Isn't this the code that I've been naively following, always putting myself last and always denying my own feelings. They taught me to behave like a martyr. I think the Catholic primary school of the 1950's wasn't such a good place for a child to be.

These reflections explain to me why I was so shocked, by advertisements in this country that declared "You are worth it" in reference to an expensive product. These are North American ideas and definitely were not part of my upbringing.

For those suffering from anxiety

If you are an anxious person, perhaps you are like Julia. She worries, overthinks things, overworks, holds in her emotions and has difficulty relating to other people, especially in a confrontation?

It's worth identifying characteristics of your behaviour that, perhaps, you have not acknowledged before. Then you can ask yourself if there are any underlying causes to the way you feel and act. For Julia recognizing the long-term effects of her upbringing is her first step towards healing.

Do you have a trauma in your background that needs to be addressed and grieved? If so this work, although difficult and painful, will give you a sense of freedom and perhaps relieve your anxieties.

Chapter 2

Struggling 'There'

1974

She is excited. She and her husband are going to move to Canada. They have completed the necessary interviews and health checks. He has just finished his postgraduate studies and she has resigned from her teaching job. It's a risk—neither of them have employment in Canada yet, but they are educated. They trust that things will work out.

They sell their bicycles, pack up everything they have into five cases and two bundles, fill a crate with the left overs to be sent later and fly across the Atlantic. After three different plane rides they arrive, collect their many pieces of baggage and go to a small, cheap central hotel that the immigration services have recommended. They're both in their mid-twenties and their new life is about to begin.

What she doesn't know is that she is trying to out-run her childhood but it doesn't work that way. Her past will come right along with her.

I'm so sad and disappointed for myself. I have a
real problem and I have to address it. I don't exactly know how. The doctor that I'm seeing is less
than helpful. Seeing Karen helps me to understand
what's going on, but I'm not sleeping any better. I'm
going round in circles. I can't work through the
anxiety of not sleeping.

I'm trying the idea of positive self-talk. I've realized
I always run myself down in my head. I've tried to
write down all the things I have going for me. It's
hard work thinking positively all the time. I recognize that I've never thought this way. I've forever
been the pessimist, protecting myself against disappointment.

One good thing is that I'm continuing to work
part time. This anchors me and gives me a purpose.
And I'm still good at work. I stay calm and work
well with the kids, but I must practise at not pushing myself too far. This is what really frightens
me—I always work too hard. I'm abusing myself in
that search for approval. Now I've got to learn to be
assertive with myself.

Observing myself is interesting. The way I hold
my head down instead of up, how I never look anyone in the eye, the way I always have to justify
myself. Karen says I need to consider my whole be-
lief system of about forty years, choose what's right

for me and disregard the rest. The thought that I might be able to do this makes me feel free.

May 8 1998

When I told Karen I was running out of positive dialogue about myself, she suggested returning to my childhood, revisiting painful things and imagining how I wish they had occurred. A kind of reprogramming. But there are so many unhappy incidents where I felt inadequate or ashamed. So many 'shoulds' imposed on me. I've decided I'll try to explore at least one incident a day.

1959

She's sitting so still in the cold room on her best behaviour. All around the edge of the room are people
sitting in hard uncomfortable chairs. She's keeping
track of all those who have come in after her. It'll be
her turn next. When the buzzer sounds, she and her
mother get up and go into the doctor's office. She
doesn't want to be here. She's been told that she
hasn't been behaving properly at home and she needs
to see the doctor. Perhaps she will need to be sent
away to a boarding school. She's very frightened this
will happen. She sits beside her mother facing the doctor. Her mother says, "I think there's something wrong
with her in the head." The doctor says "You mean..."
then points his finger to the side of his head and
twirls it around. "Oh no" her mother says, "she just
never does what she's told". The doctor checks her
ears, her eyes and her heart rate then asks a few
questions. He tells her to leave and sit in the waiting
room. She feels crushed and worthless as she waits
for her mother. She's close to tears. When her mother
comes out, they leave. Nothing is ever said about her
visit to the doctor.

Writing about childhood experiences, then trying
to give them a positive slant, brings up all the old,
painful hurts. I'm angry at my mother again. Why
was I taught that I didn't have a right to my feelings? Today, thankfully, I seem to have resolved
that a little and I'm not so angry.

I'm much better today. I think because I have taken
care of myself and have not been trying to do so
much. My sadness comes when I put my needs second. I've also learned that behind anger is fear.
Most of the time, when I get angry it's because I
have the fear that I'm being exploited, or fear I will
be hurt. I have such a hard time standing up for
myself. As I build my self-respect, I hope my anger
will subside.

As I deal with the kids at school, I'm finding a
new respect for those that stand up for themselves,
however misplaced. Surely this is healthier behaviour. I never did this, I did exactly what I was told.
I lost faith in my instincts and feelings.

The loss of my identity for so long is very sad. After
never having been my own person, its hard to develop a sense of self. My being has been so suppressed. Its healthy to grieve this, then perhaps I
can move on to recognize what I want and make
some changes. And I am making changes, I'm slowly

developing skills in dealing with confrontations. I'm trying to express my opinion in a cool, calm way.

June 25 1998

Today, I was upset again at therapy as I told Karen that I had no one that I trusted as a child. My sisters were much older, my dad never there, my mother discounted my feelings and my grandfather hardly tolerated children. So sad and alone.

1959

She's sitting in the living room playing solitaire. She's sitting in a heavy padded chair with wooden arms and she's rocking it back onto its back legs and then forward to all four legs. It helps her think about the game. Her feet are under a bar at the front giving her the leverage she needs. Suddenly the chair pitches forward and the bar crushes onto the backs of her ankles hard. She turns her head to the right as she is about to cry out and there is her grandfather holding the chair forward glaring at her. He lets go and the chair goes back onto all fours. She knows she can't say anything even though the backs of her ankles hurt a lot.

July 5 1998

I feel so awkward around people but I'm trying to open up, to socialize and I'm trying not to be so task orientated, to do the things that I enjoy first instead of last. These are all small steps towards change but I find them hard to do.

July 7 1998

I am beginning to let go of all those childhood hurts, they're just not as painful any more. It's calming to accept this past of mine. These things happened, but there was no real malice behind them. They were just precipitated by the pressures on the adults around me. Its freeing to realize that there is no reason for me to feel ashamed, I was just a sensitive child that got caught up in the British upbringing of the fifties. I can move forward now and be freer although I'm sure there will still be times that I feel sorrow for myself.

But now I'm incredibly angry about my boy-friend in my teens.

1967

She's got a Saturday job as a cashier in a bicycle/car store. She's proud of herself as there were thirty applicants and they only hired two of them to be cashiers. All the service staff are male, some of them high school students who have got themselves a Saturday job, just like her. She enjoys the work and interacting with the guys. At the end of the day, she sees her boyfriend outside pacing up and down. He's frowning and his arms are crossed. She begins to feel apprehensive. The moment she gets outside she is assailed by his angry voice. "I told that 'young one' to leave you alone or I'll thump him!" She's embarrassed, puts her head down and protests that the 'young one' wasn't anywhere near her. They start walking quickly away down a small side street. There is no one around. He berates her for interacting with the guys. "Don't let me catch you flirting with any of them!" She's ashamed and upset by his behaviour, but doesn't say anything.

How did it get to that? How did I allow his behaviour?

As a teenager I so wanted a boyfriend, so wanted to fit in. I was insecure and naive. He was older than me and at first made me feel special. He was attentive with lots of presents of chocolates and little things. Also, he would take me out to the movies and to meals. He always paid because he was out working. When I finished school in the afternoons he'd always come and meet me and walk me home and often he would phone me in the evenings.

But slowly he started to isolate me from my friends by telling me that I shouldn't spend time with them. He'd accuse them of doing this or that, which of course, was unacceptable. He also tried to discredit my family by telling me what was wrong with my sisters and my parents. He claimed he was the only one who cared about me. He had jealous outbursts if he saw me talking to any boys and then he'd tell me it was only because he loved me so much. Later he belittled me with verbal attacks and finally started pushing or hitting me if he didn't like the way I acted. He was always so sorry, I accepted his apologies and never drew any boundaries, I'd been so isolated, had such low self esteem. I didn't know where to begin.

I know now that this is the classic progression that occurs in abuse. Men and women need to be educated to recognize this behaviour and know

how destructive it can be. Women need to be encouraged to walk away early in the relationship
before things escalate. Thankfully I did get free
when I went to university. But I nearly didn't go—
he put so much pressure on me not to go, but
thankfully two older women from my summer job
encouraged me not to miss that chance. So did the
Headmistress of my old school. When it was clear
that I was going to go he insisted that I take his
ring with me to show I was spoken for.

1968

She's sitting on an airplane feeling incredible excited. She's going to university, but she's not happy about the ring in her pocket. She really wants to be free and have a fresh start. The first week is such a whirlwind of activity and she's loving it. This place has given her confidence. She knows the ring has to go back. Perhaps he gave it to her because he thought he might lose her. He was right.

What would my life had been like if I hadn't gone? I dread to think. I'm angry at myself, but I have to forgive myself for thinking that having a boy-friend, any boyfriend, was so important. I had such limited emotional experience that I was unable to protect myself. Also, I'm intensely angry with him for thinking that he had the right to hit me and try to control me. So often the question is asked "Why do women stay in this situation?" and we forget to ask, "Why would a man hit a woman he says he loves?"

After Julia tells Karen about her boyfriend Karen tries to offer another perspective. "You know, you did leave this boyfriend."

"Only because I went to university."

"Yes, but you decided to go to university, even though he was pressuring you not to. You listened to your inner voice. Keep listening to it, it will give you a sense of what's right and what's wrong for you."

Julia nods. Her self-esteem is very low. It's a pity she had no one to confide in when she was younger. She has held on to this trauma too long.

Karen adds, "And forgive yourself. As a teenager, with your background, you were very vulnerable. Abusers develop excellent skills at finding those vulnerable and manipulating them. Often, the abusers themselves, have such a feeling of inferiority, that they need to control someone else to boost their self-esteem."

Julia understands this but still feels anger towards him.

"It may help you if you write him a letter expressing all your feelings that weigh you down. You won't send the letter so you can say anything you like. It's a way of validating yourself and letting go."

I'm following up on Karen's suggestion that I write my boyfriend an unsent letter to release some of my feelings. My letter is just spitting with anger, I can feel my anxiety rise just thinking about him. I've buried all of this deeply, without even acknowledging how hurt I was. Now I just want to meet him in a bar, throw his beer all over him and belittle him the way he used to do to me.

July 10 1998

We've got a chance to go to Europe for two weeks. It's a great deal, but I'm scared and anxious. My mind is full of worries about not sleeping if we do go. Why do things continue to be so difficult for me?

Karen really helped me today. She suggested that if I had problems in Europe, we could always go over to England where I feel more comfortable. One sentence relieved all my anxiety, I felt it flooding out of me. I realized I was so scared of being trapped in a situation that I couldn't control. Feeling out of control, that's what the anxiety is all about. All my life I've always worked towards controlling everything (as if anyone can do that), instead of having confidence in myself that I will be able to cope with the unknown.

July 11

I've always had difficulty making decisions, but that's because I've always believed that a decision was final and that it couldn't be changed. I'm learning to keep my options open before I commit to a decision and that decisions can be changed. I have to trust myself to do this when I need to, instead of trapping myself into situations.

I remember spending ages trying to choose between two pictures for the house. Eventually I chose one, took it home and held it against the wall. Immediately I 'knew' it wasn't right. (So I do have some instincts!) After anguishing about it overnight I decided that I would try and take the picture back. I was amazed that the store was more than happy to make the exchange for the second picture. Who knew it was that easy? How many other things do I make difficult for myself?

When Julia tells Karen about the paintings, Karen smiles. "You are beginning to trust yourself, that's a good step forward. Keep practising those kinds of interactions with the world. Each success will help you to free yourself from that fear of being exploited or hurt. But be kind to yourself, don't expect to be perfect every time. Remember mistakes are a chance to learn. We can always talk about them here."

Julia feels more relaxed and positive. "Thanks for your help Karen."

"And remember, change takes time," Karen adds.

1962

It's her mother's birthday. She wants to surprise her
by getting her some nozzles for her icing cake set but
she needs to know which ones her mother already has.
It's morning, she's only got that afternoon after school
to shop. She asks her Mum to leave the kitchen for a
few minutes but doesn't give her a reason. But her
Mum is busy and refuses to leave. She gets upset,
she's almost crying and she is jumping up and down.
She tells her Mum, please, leave just for a minute. Her
mother leaves in exasperation but her Granddad, who's
in the room, gets up and stands in front of her with a
horrible look on his face. He growls at her and tells
her what an awful child she is. She's frightened but
she dodges past him and checks the cupboard quickly.
But the surprise is spoiled. Now, all she feels is shame
about how she behaved.

July 13 1998

This anxiety about my sleep has certainly got my attention. I've been seeing a naturopath/ homeo-path for several months now. He says his remedies will help to calm me down and that antidepres-sants would upset my body's balance. But things are still so difficult for me I've decided to see my doctor to discuss taking antidepressants. I don't trust them, but something has to change. I can't continue with this level of anxiety about my sleep.

August 10 1998

I found seeing the doctor very difficult. He didn't acknowledge my low energy levels and didn't counsel me through my fears of medication. I needed his support but he just prescribed the anti-depressant. Karen suggested that I listen to myself and consider finding myself a new doctor who is more sympathetic to my problems. She's right, but how do I find a doctor that I trust?

August 15 1998

Reading over my journal makes me realize that per-haps I do have more of a sense of myself than I thought. Initially I had difficulty sifting through things and finding my way; I would turn every which way for advice. But I did eventually slowly form my own opinion. The problem is, I get very up-set if someone contradicts me, puts me down or disa-grees with me, I shrink into myself and feel like cry-ing. I was like that with the doctor and now I feel very unsure about taking the antidepressants.

As Julia sits in that comfortable chair, Karen asks, "And so, what about the antidepressants?"

"No, they are not for me. Do you know what that stuff does? I won't be able to be myself."

"Well, I don't think they change who you are. But they do help soften the intensity of the emotions."

"I'm seeing a naturopath/ homeopath who says he has natural remedies that can help me. It just takes time for the body to adjust. I'm not prepared to experiment with the antidepressants. It might take six months to find one that works for me and during that time I'll have to suffer all the side effects."

Karen lowers her head. She's explained to Julia that as a therapist it's not her role to change her clients' minds, only to make relevant suggestions and ask relevant questions. That is important for a trust relationship.

Julia is making a decision very common to those with mental illness. She is rejecting the medication for the reasons that she told Karen. But there may be something else at work too; perhaps Julia hasn't reached the point where she can admit that she is mentally ill. She needs to cling to the illusion that there is nothing seriously wrong with her. She still believes she can get well on her own. Denying her needs is a behaviour that Julia has perfected over many years without realizing it.

For those suffering from anxiety

If you are one of those people who gets anxious because you feel you cannot control your surroundings, it is helpful to realize that no-one can totally control their surroundings. The solution is to develop confidence in yourself so that you feel capable of dealing with sudden changes around you. How do you do this?

Julia did this kind of work by praising herself for all the little things that she did to help herself. She tried to stop any negative inner dialogue. Succeeding with that gave her a sense of achievement. She also wrote unsent letters to those who had harmed her. This was a powerful way of giving her a voice, boosting her self-esteem and helping her to develop a sense of who she was. Perhaps these ideas could help you.

If you have been abused, realize that abusive people, like bullies, often have feelings of inadequacies themselves. They need to feel that the other person is under their control. Their classic behaviour is to isolate the victim from their friends and family, to verbally criticize them and finally to resort to violence to exert their control.

If you get very anxious in certain situations, or if you have generalized anxiety, you will probably be faced with the decision of whether to take antidepressants or not. Julia could not commit to antidepressants at this point in her story, as she felt that she would lose control of her real self. But you can choose your own path.

Give the antidepressants careful consideration and listen to your doctor. Ask about which medication would be best for you and how long you would have to take it. Find out as much as you can before you make your decision, but know that you are likely to feel much more comfortable if you do take the right medication. Then you will have more energy to work on the other aspects of your healing.

Chapter 3

Some Discoveries

"You know," says Julia, "I'm glad I'm continuing to see you, Karen."

Karen tips her head to the side, a characteristic move of hers. "Why's that?"

"You give me lots of positive suggestions that help me do things for myself. And I like your questions. They make me think."

"I'm glad you feel that way. How is your anxiety these days?"

"It's still there, I have some terrible nights sometimes but I also have lots of things to work on from my past. This distracts me and gives me a focus other than the anxiety. Even some positive memories are surfacing."

"That's good. It shows you moving forward in understanding of yourself."

1961

She is sitting in a dim drafty entrance hallway. Beside
her sits her mother. There's no conversation and she is
nervous. Her name is called, she and her mother follow
the caller down a wide, high-ceilinged, silent corridor
into a large bright room that looks over the sports
fields. This is the headmistress's office and she is
here for an interview because of the standing she
achieved in the state examination called the Eleven
Plus. Whether she goes to this school depends on the
outcome of the interview. She is shy and very tentative at first, but she is sure about her answers, especially to the mathematics questions. When they leave,
her mother seems pleased. Because of the results of
this interview, she gains a place in the Grammar school,
an institution that has a mission to provide girls with
an academic education that may lead to post-secondary
studies.

August 22 1998

I've been reading 'Emotional Intelligences' by Daniel Goleman. No wonder I was confused as a child. With my background of doing what I was told and suppressing my feelings, I didn't develop much emotional intelligence. I had a hard time getting on with other kids. I didn't react spontaneously to situations and no one could get close to me. Since I didn't feel able to stand up for myself, others took advantage of me further increasing my bewilderment. I was so insecure.

I'm still like this. I need to listen to my internal reactions and express them. I need to say no, say what I think, learn to respect myself—then others will respect me. These are skills that will free me from my insecurities. I'll no longer be a victim of other people's desires. Pleasing others is not worth the turmoil of suppressing myself. I need to feel that I have the right to advocate for myself.

August 23 1998

Last night I woke and started thinking about friends and how I've never let people get close to me. At University I had a strong friendship with Janet to the exclusion of others. She was such an outgoing, fun person, but she slowly undermined me with subtle criticisms and betrayed the confidences that I shared with her. And this has happened a number of times since. I've made friends with outgoing people whom I admired only to be

49

disappointed and hurt later when they took advantage of me.

I guess I've built up a lot of walls to protect myself from this happening again. I have to work at these feelings, make better choices about friends. Friendships are so important, its worth taking time to nurture them. Instead of keeping things hidden and pretending that everything is perfect, I could be more honest, telling others that I trust, how I'm struggling. Basing a friendship on truth is a good thing.

August 23 1998

So much keeps coming up, there's so much to write about.

1980

She is lying on a bed partly sitting up. She's holding her breath and pushing with all her might. Her husband is whispering for her to breathe but she ignores him. Her body has to do this, she is enveloped by the feeling. She's in pain but she doesn't care she is overwhelmed by this need to push. Their incredible son is born. She feels like the cleverest person in the world. About two years later she does the same thing and their beautiful daughter is born. She has never had a great desire for children but she is amazed by her maternal instinct. She would do anything to protect these kids.

I realize I parented the way I was parented. I swore I would never hit my kids after my experiences as a child but I never understood until now that I was a controlling parent. I feel I've undervalued my son, that I've caused the same feelings in him that I experienced as a child. This thought is heartbreaking. How am I going to deal with this?

As a parent, I was too critical and rigid in my ideas and did not praise and support him enough. I lost my temper with him and undermined him with words. He was the first child and I had such unrealistically high standards. I need to talk to him about this but it's so difficult to engage him.

My daughter had an easier time, my ideals were more realistic by then. Besides that, she was never a compliant child like my son. If she didn't want to do something she'd scream and scream until she threw up. I had to work around that.

This is a big one for me. It tears me apart to think that I may have caused my children distress. I have to put this right as best I can so the controlling legacy doesn't get passed on.

1998

She's sitting watching afternoon television with her daughter. Dr Phil is counselling a mother and daughter. In his opinion the mother 'smothers' her daughter. She turns from the television. "I don't smother you do I?" She is taken aback when her daughter rolls her eyes and nods.

I've written both my kids letters. Letters to apologize for my faults and to encourage them to be who they are. I really want them to be free of my mistakes.

These letters are important to me, they put things in perspective. They give me a chance to air my feelings of inadequacy and allow me to reflect on how I can interact with my kids in a better way. Acknowledging my feelings to the kids seems to be freeing me.

Although I'd put my heart and soul into these letters, neither of them seemed to pay the letters much attention or think of my parenting as a big deal. I hope this is a good sign. I must be careful not to expect them to be more adult than they are. They are just kids and they don't need to know about all my problems and soul searching. I need to be there for them, not the other way round. Thankfully, in retrospect, I realize that I always fiercely defended my kids if I thought they needed me. I had such strength if it was on their behalf.

1985

Her dad is furious with her son, she knows that look, she hasn't seen it in years. He's going to hit out. She's not going to let this happen, he's not going to hurt her son. They are standing on the stairs. She moves quickly to stand between her son and her father.

She asks her father what's the matter.

He tries to move round her to get at the boy, but she keeps her body in the way and looks him in the eye. She's so frightened, but whatever, she won't let him touch her son.

Finally, he steps back and the threat dissipates. She's made progress, her dad has stepped down. Her child is safe for now.

August 26 1998

Generally, this week I've been feeling more positive,
I'm taking care of myself better and socializing
more. This is a great step forward.

September 3 1998

Fearful thinking about the future doesn't help me,
it just wastes energy. Often events never come to
pass. There are no guarantees that everything will
always be alright, so I need to trust myself to deal
with difficulties when they arise. I will overcome
my fears by taking risks. Each day I must ask myself, 'What risk am I going to take today?'

September 28 1998

Karen says I've got to stop trying to control my
sleeping because its beyond my control. The mental
anxiety and fear that this creates exhausts me and
takes away my peace of mind. I don't have to think
this way. But I know I have to sleep and this is the
dilemma for me.

October 12 1998

I'm not really very ill, it's just the stuff that goes on
in my head that drags me down. Karen says I have
to learn to think differently but that's not so easy. I
keep defaulting to the old patterns. My insecurities
come up and consume me and my mind harms me.
It worries and re-analyses little things all the time.
It goes on and on and won't let go. Maybe I should
do this. Maybe I should do that. What's right?

What's wrong? The worry is centred on fear that things won't work out. I have so screwed up, I am so screwed up, I'm lost, I can't get out of this. I try so hard to do things right, to get better.

1960

She's out in the small orchard tipping the contents of the pot onto the ground. She's devastated. She'd offered to bring a small Christmas tree to class. She'd gone out and cut some branches off an evergreen tree and then potted them. She'd arranged them just so and then spent ages covering match boxes to make little presents to hang on the tree. She was so proud of her tree as she'd carried it to school. When she came back from lunch break her tree was no longer in the classroom. She was told it had been thrown outside. She tearfully asked the teacher why, then one of the girls came forward and, in an angry tone, said, "It isn't even a Christmas tree, just a few branches. And the presents aren't real!" The teacher looked around the class and said, "Since everyone is so upset perhaps you should take the tree home again." She doesn't understand. She tried so hard to do something nice for the class, she doesn't know why her tree is no good. Their Christmas tree at home was always made from cut branches. She feels stupid, a failure, so much an outsider and takes the small tree home. She quietly creeps into the orchard, so no one will see her, and tips her tree out.

I need to work on my overreactions. Just little
things can set me off. My problem is I don't trust
myself to get out of a tough situation, so I put tremendous pressure on myself to do things perfectly
the first time round. I am constraining myself so
much. This box of perfection is an exhausting
place to be. And I'm so critical of other people if
they don't do things as they 'should'. Perhaps that's
what's so hard on me, I fear other people will judge
me the way I judge them. I have to accept we all
make mistakes, but I am so obsessed with being
perfect. I never think, You rarely make mistakes.
You are very capable. It's not part of my internal
messaging. Perhaps it should be. I need to purposely
make mistakes, take risks, to show myself that I can
solve the resulting situation. Then something new
won't petrify me so much.

1958

She is reading out her report card in the kitchen. She is proud of it. School is something that she is doing right. Her grandfather comes in and brusquely tells her to stop being so boastful, no-one wants to hear her praising herself. She is immediately quiet and feels ashamed. She is still not doing things right.

I realize I use anger as a justification to express myself. I don't need this. I just need to calmly think out my point of view and express it. My inner voice is usually very accurate. Now I need to honour it. By expressing myself I can find my identity, stop being so submissive and relate better to others. Perhaps this will help to free myself from some of my protective behaviours that have dictated my life and I can say goodbye to powerlessness.

At school, I'm going to engage the kids more in helping with the day-to-day classroom things. They can collect papers, hand out materials and run the audio-visual equipment. This would help me. I wouldn't have to do so much and it would involve them more in the classroom. Generally teaching keeps me engaged, stops me from thinking about how I can't sleep.

I realize that I can identify those students who are having emotional difficulties so easily. Their haunted look, the tilt of their head, how they keep to themselves. These kids are lonely. I so hope that they have someone to talk to. In my own way I do try to encourage and support them.

I remember as a child being so isolated and often turning to our pet cats for comfort. They always came and sat with me when I was upset. They never hurt me the way the adults did. I guess that's why I like cats so much today.

1957

She's sitting on her own, on an old dusty staircase, the back staircase in an old house way out in the country. There is a great depth of sadness and loneliness surrounding her. But sitting on her lap, purring is a black and white cat. The cat always has time for her especially if she's gentle and kind. It even sneaks up onto her bed at night, although if it's caught it's put outside. And it always comes to sleep with her if she's sick. She feels a great sense of comfort in the presence of the cat. It always accepts her exactly the way she is. It's reliable, she can trust it, its behaviour is consistent, it never lashes out unless it's provoked.

I was never told I was loved. That was hard. I thought it was all my fault because I did not live up to their expectations. I think that by ten I'd learned that my real self was not of any value and should be hidden. I have to counter that now. I am worthy of love. I need to be less critical of myself. I've made a lot of small changes, I shall keep making little changes until I've developed into a much stronger healthier person.

It's interesting to see how my inner child was held down and how these restraints of old are trying to keep me there. I'm determined to get out. I will keep negating all that programming that causes me hardship. It just shows how far reaching a child's upbringing can be. I heard an interview by Elton John about his childhood in the fifties and sixties and how it's taken the best part of his life to recover. So similar, so British.

I get frightened and anxious for no reason. The thought of any kind of confrontation scares me. Is it because I used to live in fear of my Dad? I was always told that if I'd just behaved properly, Dad wouldn't have lost his temper and wouldn't have hit me. This is the reason why I always try to control everything about myself. But I can't control everything, I'm exhausting myself trying. I'm just mimicking the behaviour of the child who was trying to survive. This has no place in my life today. I just need to find my confidence.

1957

She's frightened of the dark. She always leaves her bedroom light on at night. She awakes one night to find her parents in her room. They need her bedside light. She can't do without her light. She starts to scream and cry and beg for them not to take it. In frustration, her father seizes her blankets and throws them out the window. He threatens to hit her if she isn't quiet. Her fear of her father replaces the fear of the dark, she curls into a ball and whimpers quietly. He leaves with the light. Her mother runs downstairs and retrieves her blankets from outside, settles her down and tells her she can't understand her. Why would she want to upset her dad so? She's ashamed, she can't tell her mother that she's frightened of the dark. She thinks her mother will tell her not to be so silly. In-stead she curls up whimpering and hides under the blankets.

October 19 1998

Asking for help is a problem for me. Do I feel I'm not worthy of help? Perhaps I don't want to be beholden to anyone. I want to get past this, leave things behind.

October 30 1998

I remember so clearly when I was in university. All my decisions were my own. It was a wonderful heady time. Even then, I had this vision that I'd been tied down by lots of threads and that I was cutting those threads. So much freedom, so much fun. But as I came near to the end of my studies I could feel those threads binding me again so I'd be ready to go out into the working world. I did it to myself. These threads need to be loosened and cut again.

November 5 1998

I've come a long way. I'm beginning to put things in perspective. Out of control times require a big breath and relaxation. I need to walk away, instead of trying to solve things. This is a hard one for me. When I feel out of control, I start trying to get all my work done so I can feel in control. Instead I need to stop my work and take a break.

Julia continues to see Karen once a month. They talk about the many things with which Julia is struggling.

"Studies show," says Karen, "that people who are abused in their formative years, have low self-esteem, difficulty with friendships, obsessions about controlling things, fear of the world and an overreaction to life around them. Do you think any of these behaviours are true for you?"

Julia feels a wave of relief. Her problems are common in an abused person. And she has already been trying to change these kinds of painful behaviours. She smiles wryly, "I guess I fit the profile."

Karen nods her head, "It's a big step forward to recognize these behaviours and their causes."

Julia feels so supported by Karen but at the same time she feels very sad for herself. "How do I get over the intense sadness, anger and pain that I feel about all of this?"

"Well, to validate your feelings you can write unsent letters to your parents, containing all your anger and hurt. Sometimes, it takes more than one letter, things can keep coming up. Later you can write letters of how you wish it could have been. This will help you in your grieving process. Does this sound like something you could do?"

Julia nods. "Is there anything else I can do?"

"You could write supportive letters to your younger self or imagine visiting her with words of comfort. The kinds of words you wish someone could have given you at the time." Karen takes a breath. "Grieving takes time, don't hurry the process. As you work on this, the sadness and anger will slowly diminish."

Again, Julia smiles. "Of course, I want results yesterday."

Karen returns the smile, "And to help yourself from day to day, write positive statements about yourself. You have lots of good attributes. You can start by praising yourself for not continuing the cycle of violence in your children. And as you feel more positive about yourself you will probably find it easier to sleep."

All the tears I did not weep
All the words I did not speak
Gathered there, I couldn't sleep
I need to speak, so I can sleep

I will break those threads that tie me down
I will find my way back to the ground

For those suffering from anxiety

Most anxieties have some underlying causes. They are rarely about what is obvious. Julia sees her anxiety as being about not sleeping, but it really goes much deeper than that. Maybe your anxiety has underlying trauma and you have behaviours that exacerbate the anxiety. If this is the case, you can get help from a therapist to expose the feelings and explore how this affects you today. Often protective behaviours are developed that have no purpose now and are actually harmful. If you have not experienced trauma, you probably still have behaviours that, unknown to you, support the anxiety. This is all part of the process of going back before you can go forward.

Perhaps you are a sensitive person like Julia and internalize hurts far more than some other people would. Sensitive people are often far more deeply affected by their environment than others. They need help dealing with past hurts and the ugliness that can surface in this changing modern world. Mental illness can so easily be triggered within them.

A powerful part of Julia's healing is writing letters directed to her past. It allows her to express all her hurts, to validate them and to grieve them. Following this, she writes letters of how she wished things had been, a way of re-framing the past. She also writes about her positive attributes. Perhaps these ideas would work for you and give you the opportunity to become a stronger, healthier person. It is a way of breaking invisible threads that tie you down.

Chapter 4

'There' is changing

December 1 1998

At first, I didn't know the reason for my journal, but it has become my touchstone. Writing relieves me of my stored emotions, allows me to be introspective and to understand myself. It gives me the hope that I can move forward. Sometimes I'm surprised by what comes out onto the page. I might not be solving my anxiety, but I am able to see so many things that have made my life harder. Yes, I'm struggling, but I have changed. I feel I know the causes of my self-abusive behaviour and that I've come to terms with a lot of things from my past. But now I have to make changes in my lifestyle and behaviour or I've wasted my time getting this far. So what must I do?

I've got to keep looking for fun things to do and not just accept a simple routine. I've got to take risks for myself and dismiss that voice that says, 'Its so much easier and more comfortable not to make the effort.' I need to socialize more and nurture my friendships.

I've got to keep up the positive internal dialogue and have confidence in myself. Then I won't become fearful and overwhelmed by my anxiety; the phrase, 'I don't have to think about that now.' is especially good for me.

I've got to stick by what I think and not acquiesce to another person's point of view. I've always questioned my judgment of situations and people, instead I have to develop confidence in my judgments and accept them as being right for me. I'm bound to make mistakes, but by trying I will learn and become more sociable. Internally, I know the uncomfortable feeling that I have when I disagree with others. I can use this awareness to listen to myself. I don't want to spend the rest of my life agreeing with others and denying my own feelings.

I've got to say NO when I'm asked to do too much. I don't have to explain myself. Others are not more important than me, even if they are in a position of authority. That's a challenge, but also an opportunity to learn. I can advocate for myself and each day, check to see if I have been ignoring myself.

I've got to stop judging people so harshly. In my head, I berate people and see what they are doing wrong. And I don't forget, I carry things for years. Perhaps its because I was judged so harshly; I have embodied that voice, first applying it to myself and then to others. Karen helps me realize that I expend a lot of wasted anger on other people, just because their behaviours are different from mine.

I've got to work at under-reacting internally. I get upset so easily over things that aren't going my way. Using the phrase, 'This isn't really important' is useful. Then, I need to forget about it by doing something I enjoy. This needs practice and I think, at first, it will cause anguish.

I've got to learn to accept praise graciously and push away the uncomfortable awkward feelings initiated by praise.

All of these ideas will help me and, over time, give me solutions to the anxiety. I wonder if all anxious or abused people get caught up in these damaging behaviour patterns.

At work, I'm going to stop eating lunch at my desk, instead I'll go to the lunch room and socialize. I suppose I work through lunch so that I can leave on time. What I'm really doing is cheating myself and pretending that I'm not overworking. I need to break this worship of work—it's really just a way of seeking approval. I am more than the work that I do. But making these changes is hard.

(There is a list and explanation of behavioural patterns common to anxious people in Appendix V)

Karen listens to Julia's list of all the things that she feels she needs to do. "That's quite a list. I'm glad you have put having fun first. So what kinds of things are fun for you?"

"I've started to do jigsaw puzzles again. I like them, they take me out of myself. Somehow, I just seem to be able to see shapes and colours that will fit in the right places. Also there's a drawing course at the local college that I might take. It's called 'So you think you can't draw' and I can't draw, so perhaps it'll be a good fit."

"Those sound like relaxing things to do and I think that's what you need. But you've got a number of things on your list that concern other people. How's that going to work for you."

Julia thinks carefully, other people are always such an unknown quantity. Interactions can cause her difficulties. "I have to look for opportunities to push myself and respond in a different way." She can already feel tension in her body as she thinks about this.

"Be gentle with yourself, know that it may not work out as expected, but don't get upset. Listen to others and try different things. You will find what works for you. Remember practice makes perfect. Although I'm not sure I should encourage you to seek perfection," jokes Karen.

"Yes, I do like to do things perfectly," quips back Julia. "But, on a more serious note, one of the things that I find very difficult, is to say 'No' to someone when they make a request of me. I always feel I have to give a reason and then they talk me out of my position."

Karen pauses, "'No,' followed by 'that won't work for me' is a very effective answer. You can back that up with, 'It's just not right for me.' This avoids having to justify yourself."

Julia tries to squirrel away those two ideas. Sometimes she feels she's the one who needs a notepad.

"And remember, working on psychological and emotion issues is exhausting, that's why its important to give yourself a break so you don't over tire yourself."

As usual, Julia feels more relaxed after receiving Karen's advice. She has the sense that she is progressing toward a healthier self.

1990

She is in the kitchen when the overhead fan/light bursts into flames. She rushes over to the light switch and keeps pushing the switch up so the light will go off. Her panic has caused her to revert to the British way of things. Light switch up, light off. Light switch down, light on.

Finally, she remembers it's the other way round in Canada and pushes the switch down. Those past ways of doing things are so much stronger. It's like a river being diverted from its original course. It takes work digging new channels and getting the water to flow in a new direction. But, under a deluge, the water reverts back to the original stream bed because the ruts are so deep.

December 12 1998

So I do have some very clear ideas of what I need to do to get better. I shall further explore meditation as I've tried it a little and enjoy the wonderful calming feeling that it brings. At times it sends me to sleep, sleep that I probably need. I do, however, have a lot of difficulty shutting down my thoughts and concentrating on just the 'now'. I need practice at this. I've borrowed some audio discs from the library. Healing will come from loving myself. This week, I saw a silver ring with a heart on it and bought it for myself to remind me to love myself.

January 17 1999

Yesterday, it came very strongly to me that I had abandoned myself as a child. If only I'd hung onto me, then I could have said 'no' and kept my integrity. That's what one of my sister's did. But as a sensitive child it was too difficult for me to go against the authority of my family. How do I get over this? I must not abandon myself now. I must continue to learn to develop and listen to my own opinions.

1961

She's feeling good, proud of herself she's climbing up the hill at the seaside. Something her parents suggested she do because she was bored. The path is pretty steep, but she keeps going. She wants to get to the top and see the view out to sea. Then she sees her dad striding after her. He's come to join her, she's sure he'll be proud that she has achieved so much. She's waving and waiting for him so they can go on together.

He reaches her, he's hot and sweaty and he's furious. "How dare you worry your Mum?! You're walking too close to the edge!"

Close to the edge? She's not close to the edge, she's following the path.

"You have to come down right now! You should be ashamed of yourself being so inconsiderate."

She's devastated, about to cry.

I'm learning to praise myself when successful. That praising really works. I'm a very nervous driver, not wanting to drive to unfamiliar places. We needed a new sofa in the basement. So I decided I would go out on my own, to the city where the furniture stores are located. Yes, I was nervous, but every step of the way I kept praising myself for just doing it, just going out into unfamiliar territory. It replaced my worried feeling and fear of not being able to do this. I bought a sofa. I felt very proud of myself. Such a change in inner dialogue.

1999

She wants to be able to drive in Britain, but that scares her, all those small roads and roundabouts. The roundabouts are especially difficult. She decides to be pro-active, so over a series of three visits to Britain, she books six driving lessons with the same instructor. This visit, she is going to rent a car at the airport and drive to her Mum's. With her new found confidence, she can do this.

I must listen to my anger and use it effectively. It tells me when things are not working for me and is a signal to change the way that I'm reacting. If I don't deal with it successfully, then I internalize it and stew over it. Later it comes bubbling out in an explosive way. I can understand my Dad's reaction to us kids now, how he lost his temper, a temper that I see in myself sometimes.

But, at times, my anger does serve a purpose. I often won't speak about issues that I'm concerned about because I don't have the courage to put forth my point of view. But if I get angry enough, I will speak out. My anger gives me a voice. But it's uncomfortable and exhausting. It would be so much better if I could state my opinion calmly, listen to the other person's opinion and then offer my counter argument. There doesn't have to be a right or wrong.

So, perhaps I can talk about women's rights, the environment and animal rights without getting upset. It would save so much of my energy. Isn't that what Karen encouraged me to do that very first session?

This week I'm going to look out for my anger, address it or let it go. Then I will be dealing with things as they come up. I know it will be difficult to change those old behaviour patterns, but I have to try. This is all so hard. I can see why it's easier to be stuck in illness, rather than do the work that is necessary to get well. Perhaps a part of me just wants to stay here, where things are familiar. But, on the other hand, I want to 'dance' freely and no longer be constrained by the tiny box into which I have put myself.

For those suffering from anxiety

A journal can be very valuable to an anxious person. It can be a way of discovering your true thoughts and feelings; a way of finding your authentic self; a way of validating your instincts; a way to put things in perspective and a way of healing. At first, Julia's entries were mainly factual and contained no emotions. But as she continued to journal, she was surprised by the depth of feelings and ideas about herself that spilled out onto the page. There was actually understanding, and sometimes wisdom in her writing.

It took Julia a long time to grieve for the past and a long time to work on ingrained behaviours that needed changing. In a way she had to go through the process of growing up and becoming an adult, instead of viewing the world with the faulty guidelines given to her child.

The thing about emotional change is that it actually changes the structure of the brain. New nerve cell pathways are formed in the brain and this takes time. So don't be impatient with yourself. It takes at least a month of consistent practice to affect a change.

Julia no longer wanted to abandon herself. To help with this, she praised herself for any small change that she made.

This positive dialogue technique is very powerful and worth trying if you feel unsure of yourself. At the very least it will boost your self esteem. With a more positive view of the world, more things will seem possible to you. You might even reduce your anxiety.

Chapter 5

Healing of some family relationships:

My Mum

March 7 1999

I need to go over to England again. Mum and Dad
are in hospital. I suddenly feel I can't cope, I'm
afraid I won't be able to sleep. But I remind myself
I mustn't get into the trap of worrying about the future. I am stronger now and more able to cope. I
need to have confidence in myself. I'll learn from
this.

March 10 1999

As I'm spiraling down, not sleeping has become
forefront in my life again. Why is that anxiety so
persistent? Traveling is a trigger but now I have
more skills to deal with it. I have to remind myself
of the changes I've made in my life. I can speak out
for myself more clearly. I can calm myself more
easily. I have a much clearer idea of who I am. I
can be okay if I go to England for a week. I can
take sleeping pills every night if I need to.

Trip to England

Monday March 15 1999

I feel so much at a loss, jet-lagged and worrying about sleep. Lying awake until I hear the dawn chorus is so upsetting. The fear I feel is not useful, it needs to stop if I'm going to stay healthy. I have a choice: I can be anxious and tired or choose to believe things will be okay and just be tired.

Tuesday March 16 1999

I have so little energy but my sisters and I are moving towards getting some support services in place for my parents. Mum is out of hospital but Dad will stay there until both of them are a little better.

Thursday March 18 1999

This trip to England has exposed another piece of the puzzle for me. I have revisited my lonely seventeen-year-old self who was struggling with friendships and boyfriend problems. A seventeen-year-old that was depressed. This has helped me realize that I had no emotional connection with my mother. I had completely shut her out. She'd always denied the validity of my thoughts and feelings, so I kept them from her. I was frightened of having my feelings rejected by her again so I never took the risk. I never had a chance to be emotionally supported because I never asked for help.

It's so sad that there should have been such a distance for so long. My parents lost me and I lost them. And, of course immigrating to Canada when I was in my twenties, was also a way of running away. I visited them and wrote letters most weeks as a dutiful daughter 'should'. But the relationship had walls around it. Without even knowing it, I had long since learned not to tell my parents anything that might upset them or anything that really mattered to me. I've stayed hidden all these years. This needed to be resolved.

As I lay in my old bedroom, I could experience all the sadness of my seventeen-year-old self who was struggling with her boyfriend but couldn't ask for help from her mother. How could I have accepted a ring from him?

1968

She's in her room at night. She's so sad. Her boyfriend
hit her again and told her how selfish she was. He said
that if she left him to go to university he'd do something terrible, maybe commit suicide. And she'd be responsible. Or perhaps he would cut her face so no-one
would look at her. She's so alone. She doesn't know
what to do. She prays not to wake up in the morning.

Today, I took a step towards healing my relationship with my mother. One of the strongest things
I've ever done. My protectiveness of my mother, that
had originally distanced me from her, argued that
she was too old and fragile now for any real talk.
But I had a strong feeling that I needed to say
something, that I might not get another chance. As
we sat at the kitchen table together, the words just
came out. I told my mother that I was very unhappy as a child. She teared up. "I must have been
a terrible mother". I tried to reassure her that this
wasn't the case. But in that moment of accepting
my words, she validated me in a way that she had
never done before. A door, that had been fast shut
for many years, was kicked open a little. We'd both
come out of hiding and exchanged some truthful
emotion. That's all we said. Oh so British.

We didn't have the chance to develop it further.
We were interrupted and I was leaving England the
next day, but it changed things for me. I had taken
a step forward. She had listened to me and didn't
deny my feelings. I know this was very painful for
her, but I really did feel that she'd gained her
daughter back, that we'd gained the beginnings of
a meaningful relationship.

My anxiety about the trip disappeared. I'd gone
there knowing that I needed to deal with some baggage, with only a vague idea as to how. I listened to
myself and helped myself feel stronger and more

confident. Now I needed to build on this step of putting the past to rest.

Back in Canada

March 23 1999

This trip was so important for me. My Mum gave me a great gift by listening. Now, my next challenge is to deal with the relationship with my father. While I was in England, I was flipping through some old family photos. I saw one of Dad when he was younger and I was immediately flooded with fear. It was still there after all these years. I am so angry at my dad for frightening me and hurting me when I was a child. I need to write him one of those unsent letters, perhaps it will settle me down. Perhaps on my next visit I'll be able to have a meaningful exchange with him.

"So tell me about your trip" Karen asks at the next session.

With happiness, Julia tells Karen all about the conversation with her Mum. She ends by saying, "You know for the first time in my life, I felt I was being real. I think I broke some of those threads that have been holding me down for so long. It felt as though in only a few minutes my life changed."

Karen listens intently, "I think this has been an important step in your healing. You received the validation that you needed. It was probably an important, although painful, step for your mother too. You have both gained back the beginnings of a relationship. I'm sure you will get opportunities to push that door open more in the future."

"Yes, I hope so. I think we have the chance of being more real with each other as time goes on."

"What would you have done if your mother had denied your feelings? That could also have been a possibility." asked Karen tentatively.

"I hope I would have been able to know that I had done my best, but I would have been very hurt. I'm so glad that didn't happen."

"Turning over stones that hide the family history can often be very painful for everyone concerned. You may get reactions that you are not expecting. It's important to be prepared for this so that your pain is not exacerbated. I am very happy this didn't happen to you. I can see that it has made you much more confident."

March 1999

Karen is pregnant. I'm going to lose her as a therapist. She has been the mirror that I needed. She's
never critical, she always supports who I am. I get
the sense that she cares about me. She has encouraged me to become my own person. I realize that
this was the support and love that I needed as a
child, that's why she has been so important to me.
Thankfully though, I will have a few more therapy
sessions with her before she leaves.

In May, Julia goes to her last session with Karen. The outer office has become a familiar waiting place with a feel of calm and quiet. In the inner office, Karen, now visibly pregnant, sits opposite her with her folder on her lap. Julia is curious as to what's in that folder, but doesn't ask.

Karen opens the folder and looks down. "I see this is our last session, I want to talk to you about abandonment issues today, since I am leaving and these are issues from your past."

Julia is surprised. "I'm not sure I see myself as abandoned in this situation."

"Even so you felt very alone as a child. It's important to talk about this so that you don't feel left alone again as our time together ends. Let's talk about the ways you feel you could have been included in your family."

1962

She is eating her dinner on her own at the kitchen table that is as big as a table tennis table. Both her sisters are out at their ballroom dancing lessons, otherwise they would be eating here too. But they are older
and out a lot. Her Mum is serving and eating dinner,
with the lodgers, in the dinning room down the hall.
Her Dad isn't home, but if he was, he'd be in the dining
room too. Usually, though, a plate is put aside for him
for when he comes home late at night. Her grandfather eats dinner in the lounge in front of the television
news, now that grandma has died. Before he used to be
with grandma in their room. As she finishes her meal,
she looks around the room and feels very lost. Perhaps
she can start her homework, until she has to help with
the dishes.

There was silence as Julia thought, "I know my parents were very busy, but I wish we'd done more things as a family. We did have a yearly family camping holiday when I was young, but still I have very few memories of us doing things together. When I was six, my eldest sister was already fourteen. Perhaps it has to do with my sisters being older than me. And I wish my Granddad had been more approachable, I can't think of any positive memories of him."

Karen listens then adds, "It's good you know what you would have liked. It's all part of the identity that you are finding."

As their session finishes Julia feels sad, but not abandoned. She knows that she will miss Karen's support. Karen recommends a number of therapists so that Julia can continue her therapy if she wishes.

For those suffering from anxiety

Is it valuable for you, as an anxious person, to spend time exploring past hurts? It can be an exhausting and painful journey. But it can also have significant rewards.

In Julia's first tentative session of therapy, she had hoped to find a solution to her anxiety within a few months. But instead, Julia's journey has led her to a place where she is dealing with her past. This is the past that caused her to behave in certain ways that have intensified her anxiety.

Self-discovery can be very hard. It delves into family history that can be hurtful to others. Julia's sister encouraged her to forget the past—she insists it's not relevant to living Julia's life now. Perhaps she's right. But to Julia there seems to be no other way forward. She needs to talk about her secrets and stop hiding.

Is Julia being selfish? Maybe, maybe not, but for her this is pivotal. As a result of her work, she has an understanding of her anxiety and has developed a new-found confidence.

Chapter 6

My Dad

1960

She's going to throw up. She's curled up moaning in the centre of the small boat. She can see some people glancing over, she prays that someone will help her. Her Dad doesn't understand how seasick she's feeling. "Stop making all this noise. People are looking. You should be ashamed of yourself!" She starts to cry. He lowers his voice. "Stop that crying! Stop it!" Her heart starts to beat a little fast. She's going into the danger zone. Her tenseness makes her crying a whimper. But there are people around—he's not going to lose it this time. She only has to contend with the seasickness.

Living with Dad was like living on shifting sand. I never knew when the ground would collapse beneath me. I never knew what was right or wrong, because the rules could change so quickly. One minute things would be fine and then suddenly everything would explode. I was constantly trying to behave in the 'right' way so this wouldn't happen.

It's clear to me, I need to make peace with Dad, even though he is slipping into dementia. I'm beginning to see him a little differently, feel more empathy towards him. I would like to establish an emotional connection with him. He worked so hard all his life to establish himself professionally. But he was always up against the British class system that strove to keep him in his place. I think he worked incredibly long hours just to prove he was worthy. He built up a great business but he was disappointed that he didn't have a son to inherit it. In his mind, to pass on the business to a daughter was never a possibility.

Mum and Dad have moved from the family home into a bungalow. My sisters have been helping them organize the move. There was so much excess furniture to be sold or given away. There were so many decisions as to the placement of the furniture that my parents kept. Now all of this is done, my

job will be to help them settle in to the new bungalow and their new community.

July 3 1999

With school over, I am off to England again. I'm
much more confident this time. I don't seem to be
too concerned about sleep. Perhaps I'll get a chance
to resolve some of my problems with Dad during
this trip.

July 7 1999

My sister called from England. Dad has had a
stroke and is in hospital. I'm so glad I'm going over
tomorrow.

July 10 1999

Dear Karen,

I imagine talking to you. You are the person
with whom I most want to share my feelings. Dad
died yesterday—my father that I feared, my father
with whom I needed to make peace. He was in
hospital following a stroke. When I visited, he was
waiting to be moved from one wing of the hospital
to another. He kept saying the bed wouldn't go out
the door. I bantered with him and got a smile
when I bet him three-pence that it would go out
through the door. I never, ever, remember joking
with him before.

This was the last conversation I had with him.
Later that evening, he died of an aortic aneurysm.

When I reached the hospital with my family, I asked for private time with him. I expected him to be laid out alone in a small room. I could do my talking, even if it was one way. But he wasn't in a private room, he was in a ward with three other living patients with just the curtains drawn round him. But I figured the patients didn't know me and they'd think I was just some crazy American woman. (Brits think that my accent is American). I had to tell him how I felt, perhaps his spirit would still be there to listen.

It must have been awful for those other patients listening, as I told my dad what I needed to say, not harshly, not accusingly. I had learned by then to understand his side of things. But I told him through tears I was so sorry we hadn't had more of a relationship. I explained, why I'd been frightened of him and how I viewed things now.

I really felt he had waited for me and given me a chance to make my connection. The experience was very cathartic; it allowed me to put a lot of demons to rest. Then I was able to support my mother lovingly, as she dealt with the death of her husband.

Something else happened that night. I was convinced I would not sleep, but I accepted it and didn't go into fear. I propped myself up in bed and stared into the darkness telling myself that it was perfectly normal not to sleep when a loved one had died. I fell asleep sitting up.

I feel I've reached some kind of milestone.

Thank you Karen, for all your help.

July 25 1999

Making connections with my Mum and Dad, has helped me in this struggle with my health. I am no longer dragged down by the heavy weight of my past. This journey has helped me to see my Dad differently. I think I am very like him. I am going to write him a letter and the next time I go over to Britain, I will burn it at his graveside.

A number of months later after leaving Karen, Julia meets a new therapist, Anna.

"Come on in," says Anna as she opens her front door.

Julia shrugs off her sweater and they go to an upstairs office. Julia sits on the couch and Anna starts with an introductory question.

"Tell me about yourself."

It's easier this time. Julia is more confident in telling her story and doesn't hold as much back as she did in the early sessions with Karen.

"I've been in therapy with Karen for over a year. I'm trying to break free of some of my English background, you know, 'the proverbial stiff upper lip' and 'everything's fine'. This behaviour from my past seems to have precipitated sleeplessness and terrible anxiety."

Julia feels this is a safe place to talk, although she doesn't talk about any of it much outside the therapy office. Her children have little idea of her struggle and she is pretty sure that none of her colleagues know anything about her anxiety problems. She still feels a welling of sadness when she talks about her parents and grandfather.

"Things were difficult for me when I was a child. I think I have come to terms with the physical abuse from my father and my mother's denial of my feelings. I thought I wasn't loved, but I now understand, that was only my perception. My father died about a month ago but I did get a chance to make my peace with him, and before that, I got a chance to open up a dialogue with my mother. I thought that was the end of my story but it isn't. At times, I still get terribly anxious about my sleep and I have a lot of internal pressure to behave in ways that are harmful to me. For instance, I still have difficulty with overworking. I think I have to finish everything, before I can relax. I'm trying to break this behaviour by purposefully leaving unfinished work at school instead of staying late to finish it, or bringing the work home. This makes me terribly uncomfortable but I hope that will get better with time."

Anna is scribbling furiously. She looks up as Julia stops, "You've told me so much about yourself and your progress. There's lots for me to take in, but it's obvious you have done good work with Karen. What is it that you feel is most important to pursue now?"

Without even having to think, Julia answers, "Anxiety and sleeplessness."

Anna nods, "I think, if you are comfortable with yourself and your life, you will be able to sleep. Maybe we need to explore things that make you uncomfortable. You say that you overwork. Why do you think you do this?"

"I just feel there are so many things that need to be done."

"Would it be so awful, if you didn't do these things?"

"Well, in some cases, yes, because there are deadlines at school." Julia sighs.

"But not everything at your work is governed by deadlines. This week, look for ways of making your job a little easier."

"I've already been doing that. I get kids to do more of the routine chores in the classroom, I mark a little less of their work and as I said I'm leaving unfinished school work at school."

"That's great. I'm glad you are already working on this. What about home? Do you overwork there?"

"Probably" says Julia, "but I'm trying not to be so serious about parenting the kids, to let a few things slide. It's really hard, because I want the best for them. I think I'm a perfectionist at heart and find it difficult to accept my mistakes."

"But mistakes show us we are human and give us opportunities to learn."

"I know, but I still don't like to make mistakes. Part of my pro-gramming, I guess."

"Well, yes, mistakes had terrible consequences for you in your past. But now mistakes are rarely that serious. Trying to be perfect all the time, though, can be more serious, it's not good for your health. So, before I see you next time, look for ways of being less than perfect, of not doing all that work that you think you have to do."

1955

She's sitting in the back of her grandfather's car. She sees her mother beckon to her from the grocery shop door. She's been sitting so still, so quiet, she's going to get her reward, a special treat, an ice cream. Just as she starts to open the door her grandfather turns, his eyes narrow. His voice is forceful. "Don't you dare move." She sits frozen with fear, with anguish. Her mother starts waving more insistently for her to come, but she can't leave the car. Her mother disappears from the door and a few minutes later returns, to the car, exasperated. "Why didn't you come in to get an ice cream when I waved? It's too late now." The child is close to tears. She's lost, caught between the demands of the two adults.

Julia continues to see Anna for a number of sessions where they talk about Julia's progress. I quite like her, thinks Julia, but she's not Karen. She doesn't seem to get to my soul the way Karen did and my anxiety isn't improving.

October 1999

At the next session Julia is frustrated. "We need to work on my anxiety and sleeplessness, it's not getting better and it's what's upsetting my life the most."

Anna looks straight at Julia and takes a deep breath, just like Karen did, when she had something important to say. "Perhaps you need to accept your sleeplessness. It may be with you for a long time."

Julia looks at Anna in horror. "How can I do that? Everyone needs to sleep!"

"Instead of fretting and trying to sleep, you could get up and do some reading or house work or journaling." continued Anna.

"But then I'd feel terrible the next day! How would I function? How would I teach? I have to believe that I'll get over this condition."

Anna tries again, "But if you accepted the sleeplessness, you'd be just tired instead of both anxious and tired."

Julia is upset. She has to overcome her sleep problems. Anna's idea feels like giving up. Sleeping well is something she must do.

Julia goes home that evening upset with the exchange. How can I believe it'll always be like this, I'm in therapy to get better! she thinks. This isn't working out. Anna's not helping me. I have to advocate for myself. Julia chooses a card showing dogs, as she knows Anna likes dogs. She writes 'I believe that I must get over my anxiety and sleeplessness. I can't see you anymore.'

A few days later the phone rings. It's Anna. "Thank you for the card, I appreciate your honesty. I understand why you feel that you can't see me anymore. But if you need further help with this I'd recommend a psychiatrist who gives individual psychotherapy and offers group therapy. This can be very helpful. He's covered by the Ontario Health Insurance Plan. You'll need a recommendation from your doctor and patience because he has a waiting list of about six months."

Julia has read a little about the successes of group therapy, but she asks herself, Do I need to continue therapy? I've faced my abusive past, acknowledged the harm it did me, recognized harmful behaviours and found ways to counter them. I've also started to use meditation daily. I love the peaceful feelings that it gives me, but it doesn't help when I really get into that anxiety about sleep. I have no skills to counter that debilitating feeling. Julia gets a referral from her doctor.

For those suffering
from anxiety

Working on relationships that matter to you, may help your self-esteem. Definitely, this was the case for Julia. But this didn't relieve her anxiety that seemed to have become ingrained into her body. She could slip into it so easily. She needed some skills to counter this kind of invasive thinking. Meditation was an excellent tool, but it wasn't enough for her. It only calmed her for short periods, she could not bring the peaceful feelings from meditation fully into her life.

Cognitive Behaviour Therapy would, perhaps, have been a good solution for her, as it teaches a person how to deal with destructive thoughts. But Julia was not aware of this kind of training. If you are interested in pursuing this, there are excellent books in the library. Also, your local Community Centre may offer evening courses in Cognitive Behaviour Therapy. It's often referred to as CBT.

Chapter 7

Back to the Beginning (almost)

In late December 1999, Julia is sitting at the kitchen table with her husband again. It is almost two years since the discussion that lead to Julia going part time.

"I know I'm only working part time, but I feel exhausted. This term has been so busy. Tomorrow during lunch break, we have another rehearsal for the skit that we're doing for the kids on the last day of school. I hope it won't take too long. And, I've still got to write one of my exams for this semester—they take forever to do. The end of the school term just can't come quickly enough for me."

"Don't worry," Len reassures her, "you've got all of the Christmas holidays to sleep."

The anxiety about sleep is still plaguing Julia, she feels as if she's just hanging on by her fingernails. Thankfully this year the Christmas holidays start early and there is some time between the end of term and Christmas itself. As soon as the term ends, Julia collapses into an exhaustion of sleep. The last two years of stress, anxiety and emotional work have taken their toll. Two days later she is supposed to collect her son from university, he's about a two-and-a-half hours drive away. She's just too tired, she can't do it. Len says he'll leave work a little early to fetch him.

Also weighing on her mind is the trip that she has booked to visit her Mum for New Year's Eve. Len has to work because of the Y2K threat—there are widespread concerns that critical computers may fail during the change over to the year 2000. She's been looking forward to all those wonderful fireworks along the Thames but she's beginning to doubt that she'll be able to see them.

Their family has a quiet Christmas, lots of presents and good food, but Julia just doesn't feel right. Then she becomes very ill with some kind of bug, perhaps the flu. She has a fever and feels terrible.

Len cancels her flight and she calls her Mum. "I'm sorry," she explains, "I just can't come."

She can hear the disappointment in her Mum's voice. "No, no, you have to look after yourself."

Julia has to drag herself to the doctor's office to get medical forms signed, so that she can get money back from her flight cancellation insurance.

For the rest of the holidays, she sleeps and sleeps. As the Christmas break comes to an end, Julia is overwhelmed by the thought of returning to school. She's fearful of not sleeping and doesn't think she can cope. This time she listens to her body, sees her doctor and gets a medical note for two weeks off work. She goes back to work briefly in mid-January to finish the school semester. But she knows she has reached her limit. She doesn't have the energy to continue to teach for the next semester. She applies, to the Board of Education, to take the next semester off work, with the intention of returning in September.

At home she asks Len if it is okay for her to move into the spare room until her exhaustion abates. "Then you won't be disturbing me when you get up early in morning and come to bed late. It's also brighter and warmer in that back room. I think it will help me."

"Sure," he says and adds, "I can move a television in there if you like."

"That's great," she says.

She collapses into a state of exhaustion, she sleeps much of the day and night. She gets up about ten in the morning and makes herself breakfast, then she goes back to bed and watches some of the morning television. Talk shows with desperate people having their lives sensationalized. It's exhausting and sends her back to sleep after about an hour. Later she gets herself a light lunch, reads a bit and then sleeps or listens to music and meditates. Occasionally she journals, but that seems to require a lot of energy, and what is there to say? 'I feel exhausted and hate wasting my life like this.'

Her daughter comes home from school at about four in the afternoon. Julia gets up to spend some time with her. They often watch an afternoon television show before her daughter starts her homework. Len comes home at six and usually cooks a meal for them. He hates to see Julia so ill. They clean up together, maybe watch about an hour of television then she goes back to bed. She never changes out of her night-clothes during the day.

Friends suggest that she might have the beginnings of chronic fatigue syndrome but she doesn't get a formal diagnosis. The medical community is still questioning the validity of this syndrome.

But slowly, slowly, she regains some of her energy, and begins to actually get dressed for the day. She takes gentle walks and starts to regain her life. She's able to do the cooking for the evening meal and do the shopping for groceries. A memory of her three months of resting is the smell of the aromatic candle that she burned in her bedroom in the afternoon sunlight.

In April 2000, Julia gets a call from the psychiatrist's office. She has been waiting for this. She is so thankful that she got the referral. It's obvious, now, that she needs more help. She books an appointment for late morning so she doesn't have to get up too early. It's a cool, rainy day when she walks, with the umbrella over her head, to his office. She slowly climbs the stairs to the upper floor. He has a receptionist who directs her to take a seat in a large spacious area. As she waits, she watches the umbrella drip water on the floor. It seems to match her dreary feeling. Yes, her expectations at the beginning regarding her anxiety were unrealistic, but now it is two years or so later and she's even worse than she was at the start of this process. She knows she will need lots of support if she is going to return to work in September.

A door off the main area opens. A small man quietly invites her into the room behind him, while nodding to the receptionist who gets up and collects a wooden chair. All three of them go into the office that has a desk and two chairs.

"I've invited Andrea to this first session. She is also a therapist and she helps me run the practice. She will listen to our conversation and check that I don't miss anything." He sits down and relaxes back into an office chair at the desk, Andrea places her chair near the window leaving a chair near the door for Julia.

It's not Karen's spacious office, she thinks, but it will do.

The psychiatrist steeples his fingers together. "So tell me, why are you here?"

This time Julia's story is a bit different. "I'm a teacher on a leave of absence for illness. I'm due to return to teaching at the beginning of the next school year in September."

"And what is your illness?"

"Well, I suffer from anxiety about sleep. I've been struggling with this for a couple of years. In late December I got some kind of bug that gave me a fever and exhaustion. Since then I've continued to feel exhausted, although it has gotten slightly better."

"Why do you think you suffer from anxiety?"

Julia has so much to say but she tries to sum it up. "I stopped sleeping properly about two years ago, then I started to get very anxious that I wouldn't get a good night's sleep. This anxiety was terrible."

"Do you still have the anxiety about sleep?'

"Not so much now, but then I don't have to get up in the morning and go to work."

"Do you like your work?"

"Yes, I do, but teaching can be very demanding. I think perhaps I was working too much."

He nods his head, glances at Andrea and says, "Tell me a little about your background"

Julia is a little bored now by questions about her past, but she knows they are important so the psychiatrist can get a better sense of her. "My Dad was physically abusive at times and my Mum always denied my emotions. I emigrated to Canada in 1974."

"And how was it to emigrate?"

"It was exciting."

1974

The Toronto autumn is bright and sunny and everything is so large, the buildings, the roads, the cars. But still, it feels like home. Canadians speak the same language and the Queen is even on their coins. It looks as if it will be easy to integrate into this society. They find themselves a little, central bachelor apartment and begin the process of getting jobs. They only have a small amount of money in reserve. She finds out that work as a teacher is closed to her because she doesn't have a year of teacher training. But she can type, she'd taken night classes a couple of years before. Within a few days she gets a job as a clerk typist. It pays more than her teaching job in Britain! Six weeks later he gets a job working in computer technology management. A few months later again, she gets a job working as a research assistant in one of the hospitals. All is good.

"You're married?" he asks.

"Yes, we got married just after finishing University. Len, my husband, continued studying to do a PhD, while I got a job teaching in a local secondary school. We came here after he completed his degree but it took me a while to get back into teaching. I had to do a year's teacher training and we didn't have the money for that at first. Then it was difficult getting a teaching position for a while. But it all worked out, I started teaching again."

1978

She graduates from teacher training in early May. She is looking for advertisements from Toronto schools but there are very few. Teachers are being declared redundant. So she gets into their second-hand, Volkswagen Beetle and goes out to the areas outside of Toronto. On her third day out, she visits a school and fortuitously the principle is looking through resumes for a teacher in her subject area. She gets interviewed there and then and a few days later is offered the job.

"We have two teenage children now. When they were little, I taught part time, but I went to work full time about ten years ago when my husband lost his job. His company was taken over by another company and he was one of the casualties. But it only took him a few months to get employed again and that's when we became very busy as a family. When all this anxiety started, I reduced my workload to part time again."

He nods his head again. "What were your dreams when you were young?"

Julia is confused, she thinks he literally means her dreams at night and thinks this is a very odd question. She shrugs her shoulders and says, "I don't really remember." Later she realizes that, of course, he meant what did she want for her life. She had wanted to be a veterinarian. but was told that veterinarians were usually men who were better at the complex sciences involved.

After a few more questions this first session comes to an end.

"We'll start meeting next week," he says. "Andrea will set up an appointment."

Julia has the feeling that she has just been interviewed for an available opening, but she is glad that she will be getting more help. Therapy with the psychiatrist offers her hope. Her illness in January has been a setback and she has lost a lot of confidence.

So begins regular therapy with the psychiatrist. He is very different from Karen. Julia notices him leaning back in his swivel chair in a relaxed way during sessions. And he never takes any notes, just listens.

Just as with Karen, the first therapy session gives her excellent advice.

First therapy sessions and some advice.

1. Deal with the underlying problems and
   your obsessions will take care of themselves.
   The underlying problem is that you try to
   control everything in your life. You have to
   learn to be more spontaneous; don't analyze.

2. Try to find time for you just to have fun.
   Give up your obsession of making lists and
   having to do things immediately. You'll
   have more energy and time.

The new thing here is that he's saying I'm obsessive. When I think about it, I realize I _am_ obsessive, although I don't want to admit it. Why does it
always take me so long to recognize a behavioural
problem? I remember a couple of years ago, when I
saw my old doctor about my sleep problems. He diagnosed me with obsessive compulsive behaviour
but I dismissed his diagnosis. I only heard what I
wanted to hear and I didn't want to consider antidepressants. Now, after checking a little, I'm finding out that obsessive behaviour partners with the
need to control everything. They are part of my
protective behaviour patterns. I'm obsessive about
sleep, health, drug side effects and wanting to have
everything completed. Perhaps I can read up on
this. (Is that being obsessive?)

Much as I've done a lot of emotional work, I still haven't let go of trying to control things. This is how I learned to protect myself as a child. When I feel secure in myself I won't need the control.

In another of Julia's early therapy sessions with the psychiatrist, he starts, "I'm finishing a new book and I'm asking my patients about their opinions. It gives me a chance to get to know them better."

Julia is immediately suspicious, I think he's more interested in trying to gather information for his book, than giving therapy. Is this really going to be a good place for me and my problems? She goes home not feeling quite so confident in him.

However, a few weeks later he says, "I think you're ready to join the group therapy that I run. I have an opening in the Thursday morning group session that takes place every week. It starts at ten o'clock and goes for about an hour and a half. How would you feel about coming?"

Julia is delighted. She's read that it can be very effective. "Yes please."

On June 1st, 2000, Julia sits in a circle of about ten people. It is bright and sunny. At one end of the group sits the psychiatrist and at the other end sits Andrea.

He begins, "Today, in the group, we have a new member, Julia, so I'll go over the rules again. Each person in group must be respectful of others and, although it has never happened, I want to remind you that physical violence is not allowed. Each time, one person will be in focus to tell their problems and everybody will get a chance to give their personal reactions. If a person doesn't feel like speaking, they can pass. At the end, Andrea will give her response and then I will sum up the situation. Think of this as a large family of siblings, Andrea is the mother and I the Father. There is one more rule. There is to be no socializing outside the group. Today, Caroline, I am going to ask you to be in focus."

Julia listens carefully to Caroline's story and then to everybody's response. She is glad that she is not asked to respond as each person seems to have a deep understanding of the problems here.

I've been going to group therapy for a few weeks now. It feels like I've come home. I'm meeting others who feel like me, struggle like me. I feel uplifted to know I'm not so alone. Sometimes I see solutions to someone's problem and then, of course, realize that I could use those solutions for me. And some of these people are on medications. I'm starting to wonder—perhaps that's not such a bad thing.

Seeing the naturopath/homeopath just hasn't been helping me. I suppose when I first started seeing him, I felt I was getting no support from conventional medicine and that a naturopath would be a good alternative. Really, I was grasping at straws. At each visit he would check my heart rate as he introduced different remedies to my wrist. He told me that changes in heart rate would tell him which remedies I needed. It all sounds a bit suspect but, for whatever reason, I trusted him, even though I have a science background.

His remedies are expensive and are not working for me. Perhaps this is an example of a vulnerable person trusting too much. I need to move on. So I've decided to talk to my new doctor about an antidepressant. She is more empathetic. It will be okay. If it doesn't work, I can always stop.

June 18 2000

When I saw the doctor about the medication she said, "You know it and I know it. You need the medication." Did I know it? Another example of taking too long to accept something that was right in front of me. Anyway, I've started on a low dose of the antidepressant and suffered through the first few weeks of side effects. They are very mild but I'm thirsty all the time. I saw the doctor again. She is very supportive and has told me the side effects will go away soon. She upped the dose and told me she'll see me in two weeks. I feel cared for and I trust her. That's what I need.

June 20 2000

So "Trust" is a big thing for me. My psychiatrist advises me to trust a person first until I have a reason not to. I've only given trust carefully and slowly, when I feel it has been earned. It's difficult to trust when you've been hurt. My background screams at me "Don't trust anyone!" I've been reading that abused people don't trust easily and are very distant with others, not sharing what is important to them and often not developing friendships. But sometimes they trust too easily, especially if the person is very gregarious and appears to be the centre of attention. They are not usually hurt by the people they push away (except for the loss of a potential friendship) but they are often badly hurt by that person who seems to promise so much and then doesn't follow through. Being let down

119

adds to the anxious person's feeling of unworthi-ness and causes them to trust even less. This has happened to me a number of times.

Also, I know I don't like to delegate to other people because I just don't trust them to do things the way I want. This leaves me overburdened. So if I could understand people better and advocate for myself, perhaps I could trust the right people, at the right time and avoid those hurtful situations which have happened to me all too often.

1958

She's playing at school in the washroom. Four of them are holding onto the toilet door so a friend can't get out. One of them slips, loses her hand hold and falls back cracking her head on the washbasin. There's a lot of blood. After the injured girl is taken away, they are asked what happened. She tells the teacher they were just playing, it was an accident. But the others put the blame on her. They say she caused her friend to let go, to crack her head. She can't believe her friends would lie like this and doesn't know what to say in her own defense.

How can I come to terms with all the injustices in the world? I am ultrasensitive and get very angry and upset when I see exploitation and mistreatment of people and animals. Don't people have a heart? How can the rich exploit the poor? Why is there human trafficking, child labour, exploitation and mistreatment of woman, children and animals? Why is there dismissal of climate change and the connection to fossil fuels? I don't see how people could ignore these problems around them. I am such an idealist, wanting to set everything right. Is that because as a child I always wanted someone to intervene for me?

1963

She's late for school. She's standing in the large
kitchen. Her mother is behind her across the room
cooking the lodgers' breakfasts. She's trying to braid
her long hair for school, but it won't go, the braid
keeps turning out a mess. She whines for help; she's
going to be late again. Her Dad comes in. He's usually
not up this time in the morning because his work keeps
him late at night. He's furious and hits her hard across
the head, across her right ear. She staggers, her head
buzzes, her ear hurts. "Be quiet! Do your own hair."
She's afraid he'll hit her again, so she does as he says.
Her hair looks awful but it doesn't matter. She hates
him. She leaves quickly, hiding the fact she's crying.
Her ear is bleeding but she refuses to wipe the blood
away. As she walks to school, it dries and cakes. She
willing someone to notice, someone to ask her about it,
but no one does.

I found out in group today that not everybody wants someone to help them. I plunged in to 'rescue' a person to whom I thought the others were giving a hard time. Funny how I can do that for someone else but not myself. But she didn't want my help. She told me it was fine, she could speak for herself. So this defense of others isn't always wanted and is not necessarily seen as admirable.

I'm so tired today, yet I'm sleeping well and I'm taking an afternoon nap. Truth be told, I'm always tired. I must check this out with the doctor. Is it the antidepressant that I've started taking, or my thinking patterns, or some physical factor causing the exhaustion?

The doctor has reassured me that I'm still adjusting to the medication, that sometimes there is tiredness at first. She also tells me that I will feel less tired as I recover from my anxiety. However she has ordered some blood tests just to be on the safe side. It's so good to have a doctor who listens to me and supports me.

Julia is waiting at the doctor's office, to check on the results, but not for long. She is always surprised at how quickly she gets in to see this doctor.

"Your blood tests are good although your cortisol levels are low. Long time anxiety can do this, that's why the antidepressants are important for you. With less anxiety and rest, those cortisol levels should return to normal. But I'm going to write a referral for an endocrinologist just in case it's more than this. It may take some time to get an appointment." This all makes sense. Julia feels so much more comfortable with this doctor.

Months later, after she has seen the specialist a number of times and the results of those blood tests have come back, the specialist assures here that there is nothing wrong with the production of her hormones. Julia asks if her exhaustion might be the result of chronic fatigue syndrome but the specialist dismisses the idea.

Meanwhile, Julia continues to enjoy going to group and now is participating by giving responses. She is always very careful because she wants to be sure she gives the 'right' response.

She enters the psychiatrist's office for her weekly session.

"So how is group going for you?"

"Good" says Julia "It helps a lot. It's good to know that others struggle with similar problems."

The psychiatrist nods his head. "The reaction you have to a person's story often has more to do with your past experiences than the actual story being told. You will feel more empathy towards those that have similar circumstances to you."

"I see," she replies.

She wants to ask if she has been responding correctly in group. She feels she needs to check that she is doing things in the right way. But, before she gets a chance to ask he says, "It's also important that you respond with how you feel. There are no right answers here. This is a place for you to practice saying what you feel."

She is a little confused, she's still caught up in her factual world of right and wrong answers even when expressing an opinion. When she goes home, she thinks a lot about what has been said.

The psychiatrist says that my reactions in group have more to do with me than the story being told. Deana tells us that when her daughter gets upset she tells her daughter that she doesn't really feel this way, that she just needs a positive outlook. It's this very daughter that is struggling with depression. I become very angry with Deana but I don't really know why. Now I realize that, from my perspective, Deana is just like my mother undermining my feelings all those years ago.

Then there's Gina who frustrates me because she doesn't lose weight. Again, from my perspective, I want her to just do what she's told, eat less and exercise more. It's easy! (Of course, encouraging a person to lose weight is a complex problem, but my mind reduces things to such black and white terms.) As a person who always did what they were told I have difficulty understanding her resistance.

And my responses—I've been struggling very hard to give the right response, to show the psychiatrist that I understand all this psychotherapy. I want him to think that I'm smart and clever. Perhaps I'm missing the point. It's about expressing what I feel. Practicing how to say what I think, without having to fear nasty consequences. Karen always said I needed to be true to myself, but in the real world it's difficult to find the opportunities. Now I have a safe place to practice this and to find my authentic voice. The language of emotion is one I'm learning to speak. I must take advantage of this opportunity.

July 30, 2000
Another trip to England

It was a success for me. I didn't have much anxiety once I was there, but I did use sleeping pills some of the time. I was able to tell my mother how important it was to me when she acknowledged that I'd been unhappy as a child. How it was helping me to move forward in my struggle to get better. I asked her what things I had done as a child that made her proud. I couldn't help tearing up when she told me she was so proud when I started ballet lessons. My Mum was a great singer and dancer when she was young yet she'd never been allowed to pursue this. But I had to pause and think. I wanted to horseback ride when I was a kid but never did. My daughter goes horseback riding now. Does she enjoy it? Or was she horseback riding because of my influence? I'll have to check this out.

Anyway, I was able to talk to my mother as an adult and give my opinions, tell her I'd always been frightened of ghosts in the large old house in which we lived as kids. When she suggested that she cut some of my long hair at the front of my head, I was able to tell her that I liked my hair as it was. I began to feel like a real person.

I also had, in my mind, unfinished business with my dad. I took the letter that I'd written to him after his death and burnt it at his graveside. This felt like a closure and a cleansing to enable me to start anew.

In August, Julia is again at a therapy session.

"So how do you feel about going back to school in September?"

"I'm very nervous about it. I'm scared that I won't be able to sleep. I can already feel some anxiety building in me. I keep thinking of what I'm going to do to cope. But I really want to do this, work is important to me."

"When a person is anxious about something, they create all kinds of scenarios in their head of what might happen and then feel overwhelmed that they can't cope. Don't do this to yourself. Have the confidence that you can cope when you return to work. Once you actually start school and face the situation, things will be easier. If you don't sleep, have the backup plan of taking sleeping pills. I can prescribe more if you need them."

Julia feels a little more relaxed. The feeling that he approves of her taking sleeping pills relieves some of her anxiety.

"Are you going back to work in the mornings or the afternoons?"

"In the mornings," Julia replies.

"Why don't you consider the afternoons then you can sleep-in in the mornings?"

But Julia is adamant, "No the mornings are best for me, then I have the afternoon to relax. I've always been the sort of person who likes to get things done and out of the way before relaxing." Julia is recognizing what she needs and advocating for herself.

August 22 2000

I'm going to be returning to work soon. This is going to be tough after seven months of not working. I'm filled with anxiety about the new school year, mainly about whether I'll be able to sleep. Old patterns never seem to go away. I wondered if I should be teaching when my health is so compromised, but teaching has been my life, it is my identity. In a way, that's so sad, but I do want to go back to work. It'll only be part-time in the mornings, so I can sleep in the afternoons. Plus I'm taking a low dose of antidepressants, I can always take more if I need to.

September 4 2000

Back to school tomorrow. We are going out to a party this afternoon. I hope it'll be a distraction for me. I'm taking the psychiatrist's advice and trying not to think of what can go wrong. I know anxiety will be running in the back of my mind, but hopefully it will be kept somewhat under wraps. Also, I shall take a sleeping pill tonight. I just have to remind myself that the beginning of the school year is a big event for many teachers and kids.

September 9 2000

I made it. The first week is done. It was hard pushing through the anxiety. And I was still somewhat anxious by the end of the week. I went to the end-of-the-week-party after school on Friday. Internally I was shaking as I tried 'to let down' after the week, but I don't think anyone was aware of it. I want to be at school, I can do this.

September 20 2000

Group beat me over the head with, "Take the sleeping pills." and the psychiatrist says, "Let go of the fight.". Just as I can't understand Gina's behaviour about weight, they can't understand my attitude about the pills. I feel such a failure whenever I take the pills. I'm going to use advice that I got a while ago: 'Go to bed, and if you are not asleep in an hour take the pills.' Then I can accept that sometimes I need help sleeping.

October 2 2000

Teaching today went well. I really am enjoying my classes. But I still give too much of myself. I make things too easy for the kids don't get them thinking and doing enough for themselves. My behaviour takes away their responsibilities and is not the best in the long run. Giving them back responsibility is one of my aims.

I realize that I always try to solve my own children's problems too. I'm not giving them the responsibility, not trusting them to do it for themselves. This evening my daughter wanted help from me with her math homework, but she started to get very snippy and rude. Instead of getting annoyed but persisting, I took a deep breath and suggested she'd better call one of her friends. Then I walked away. It was hard for me, but for the first time I made it clear that I needed respect from her if I was going to help her. I set a boundary.

On October 20th, Julia is sitting waiting for her appointment. Last week the psychiatrist had asked her to bring in a page of her journal from that week. He said he would photocopy it and put it in her file. She is clutching a page from her loose-leaf journal in her hand. I'm so much better at journaling in a meaningful way now, she thinks. I hope he likes it.

Once she is sitting in the Office, she passes it over to him. "I've brought in a page of my journal."

He leans back in his chair and reads it. She sits quietly in anticipation.

"Right," he says. "Let me photocopy this." When he returns, he hands back her page and puts the copy on his desk. He then says "How has school been this week?"

But I didn't write about that, Julia thinks. She is confused but says nothing. She can feel the disappointment rise in her. It's just another journal entry to him. I wanted him to acknowledge my journal. I wanted to talk about some of the things that I'd written about.

As the session continues, she feels that they are talking about things that are not all that important to her but she doesn't say anything. On her walk home, she thinks, He is just gathering journal entries for information for his books. I don't want to take any more of my journals to him.

Reading books about anxiety has really helped me. It helps me to see things from another perspective and to apply these ideas to my own life. I often have an explosion of thought following a book. But I must be careful not to go overboard, not to make reading these books an obsession in my journey to get well.

Why do I suffer from anxiety but my sisters do not? Our background was the same. Perhaps there is a genetic component for me. My sister tells me she remembers Grandmother sitting and shaking, while holding a book upside down. And our mother had panic attacks in her early 70's. I was and am a sensitive person which adds to my vulnerability. Perhaps emigrating to another country has been a factor too, although my middle sister emigrated to the States without any anxiety.

When I came to Canada, I already had problems with suppressing my identity in an effort to please others. Added to this, were the efforts to adapt to a different culture and fit in. It was a challenge. At first Canada seemed the same as Britain, but it's not. People are far more open with their comments, their feelings and their actions. The language has so many words that have different meanings and cause misunderstandings. And there are so many little behavioural nuances that are different. No wonder I feel there is a disconnect with my environment. I think I will always be living in the mid–Atlantic not quite belonging to either culture.

December 8, 2000

Up until now I've felt the sessions with this psychiatrist were a dance, where I had to search for meaning from a few scant words as we talked about all kinds of things that seemed unrelated to me. But this last therapy session was so helpful. It was the first time that I felt my therapy was moving forward.

This time he was more direct about some of my responses in group. I immediately felt criticized, and that I'd lost credibility with one of the group members. I had a strong impulse to put things right, regain my integrity. As we talked and I struggled to see what I could say in the next group to resolve things. I began to get very uptight. He pushed me further suggesting that my strategies wouldn't work, then I suddenly realize, that it didn't matter. Group isn't an ongoing part of my life. I didn't have to put things right or explain myself. All the tension flowed out of me. When I think of all the times that I have unsuccessfully tried to smooth things over with a person and then worried about it, I realize I need to let some things go. Not all mistakes can be corrected. I feel empowered!

December 10, 2000

I'm beginning to think that my subconscious stores lots of things from which I can learn. When I don't sleep it may be because there is something deep down trying to get out. An agitation beyond my grasp. If I can listen to my sleeplessness and relax, the wisdom will emerge. Maybe a dream, a feeling or an action, will surface and give me understanding and freedom. Dreams, especially just before I wake, seem to have lots to say to me.

December 15, 2000

Today my psychiatrist said, "You carry a lot of hidden anger." I thought I had dispelled most of my anger. I wish he had told me this before so I could have been working on it. On reflection, I have to admit that I do have an anger deep down that can explode out onto the surface when I'm pushed. I get angry when people don't do what they are 'supposed' to do, I get angry with people who don't agree with me—especially about the injustices in the world or political views—and I get angry with my own kids. Now I understand my Dad a bit more—did he have to struggle with this? But most of all I am angry at myself for losing my identity behind the facade of pleasing people. I have to forgive myself.

December 29, 2000

I am getting better, I know it. I can see it in my journal, I have so much more understanding of the world around me. Is it the antidepressant or my emotional work? Perhaps a little of both. I seem less centered on my anxiety and more involved with the world around me. I feel a little more balanced.

For those suffering
from anxiety

It is very common for abused or anxious people to have trust issues. They are suspicious of the intentions of others but sometimes they can trust too easily. Is this the case for you? It takes
time and a lot of understanding to be able to know who is trust-
worthy and who is not.

Being part of group therapy is a very powerful way of getting in touch with your feelings. If you, as an anxious person,
get the opportunity to participate in this kind of group, go for it.
Not only does it help you to feel less alone, but it also allows
you to identify and express your own feelings in a safe environment.

The group helped Julia to realize that sleeping pills and antidepressants were useful tools in overcoming her mental problems. She was however, very careful about the sleeping pills;
she'd read they are addictive so she believed that if she took
them regularly over time she would need higher and higher
doses, and then eventually they might not work at all. Antidepressants, however, are not addictive. Once an effective dose is
reached it usually does not need to be increased. However, the
body does become dependent on antidepressants to function
normally, so they should never be stopped abruptly—instead
the dosage must be gradually reduced.

After a month or so of using the antidepressants, Julia did
feel a little calmer but because she had been in such deep anxiety she didn't realize that the pills were only taking the edge off
her intense feelings. She didn't acknowledge that she needed a
higher dose for the antidepressant to be fully effective. Instead
she kept herself on the lowest dose possible.

Chapter 8

Slowly moving forward

Julia continues to go to therapy and group for the years 2001 and 2002, although now, she goes to an evening group because of her work schedule. Some long-term members of the group leave and new members come in. Julia understands herself more and can avoid some of the debilitating anxiety by occasionally taking sleeping pills. She really likes going to the group.

The people there have great things to say from which I can learn, she thinks. But she is getting upset with the psychiatrist. He never gives me the empathy that Karen did. Last week we talked a little about my dad and he asked me to write some things to continue in the next session, but in that next session he didn't even ask about Dad.

She is frustrated, especially, after a session where they spent the whole time talking about the Sunni and Shiite problems in Iraq. She stumbles down the stairs in tears afterward. I've been listening carefully for the 'moral of the story' but I can't see anything relevant to me. I'm confused. Where is the focus on solving my anxiety?

On September 13th 2002 Julia enters the office determined to talk about the direction of her therapy.

"I want to talk to you about our therapy sessions. I don't feel we are moving forward to solve my anxiety. Plus, I really need to feel that you hear me, to feel validated."

He nods his head. "You think there is a direct route to solving your anxiety. You're in a hurry. But we need to explore your reactions to the world to understand your anxiety and that takes time."

"But you don't push me like you did that one time earlier when I was having a problem with a group member. I need that push."

He picks up a small wooden ornament from the shelf, puts it on the edge of the desk and pushes it so it falls. "See," he says "no harm done. But if that ornament was made of glass, it would break when it hit the ground. You are that glass ornament. You are fragile. I have to be careful."

Julia thinks defensively, I'm not fragile. But then she feels sad as she realizes that she does get upset very easily. This world, she thinks, causes such anguish.

I've been assessing how far I've come in this journey and how I've managed to navigate this difficult pathway of anxiety. I realize that, all the way through this, my kids have had a profound affect on me. These reflections inspired me to write the following short passage.

1998

I can't sleep, I can't sleep, I can't sleep. I must sleep, I must, I must. I have so much to do tomorrow. I can't cope, my life's falling apart, what can I do? I can't sleep, I can't sleep, I'm exhausted. I'm spiralling out of control. I can't solve this, I can't sleep, no-one can help. They all sit there so placidly. They don't get it. I can't sleep. The anguish. I can't cope. I'm failing, I'm falling. Why don't they help? They're supposed to. I'm spinning and spinning. The anxiety drags me down and down and down. I'm falling and falling. I'll never get out. Always in a deep pit, no solutions, no way out, the sides too steep. I'm struggling and struggling, I climb a little and fall back further, the exhaustion. It's got to stop. I can't do this anymore, please let me sleep. I live in fear, all-consuming fear. I can't do this anymore, I can't, I can't. Make it stop, make it stop, make it stop. Please God make it stop, let me be normal, let me sleep. Let me sleep forever, stop the pain, make it stop. Let me go away.

But there are golden threads that hold me down, make me stay. I can't break these thread as I have others. They're too young to cope, they still need me, I have to hang on. I'll be free later on. Now I have to make it, I have to struggle to be normal, to cope. How will I do this? I don't know, I don't know.

2002

They saved me without knowing it. But I did it too. I had the strength to struggle, even though it exhausted me, anguished me, tore me apart, opened the flood gates to all the pain, the pain that still saddens my life. But now I can cope, I can sleep better, I can help myself. I don't ever want to live with that fear and anguish again, although my behaviour draws me there, wants me back in my place, the place that almost killed me.

Today I shared this writing with group. A risk for me, so it was reassuring to be accepted and validated. I still strive for this. This writing summed up how important my children were to me. We all need that feeling of being needed.

My psychiatrist has suggested to me that he see each member of my family so he can get a better idea of the family dynamics. My son came in first. He was calm and cool and answered all the questions easily. When asked what he thought about me teaching, he told the therapist that I obviously liked it because of the stories that I shared at the dinner table.

My daughter was a whole different matter. She didn't want to be there and let us know it. She sat back swinging her legs with a look of scorn on her face. I think she felt threatened, that she thought the session was about her. She was very noncommittal in her answers, often just shrugging her shoulders. When we left I had to reassure her that this visit was about my problems and not about her.

I don't think he got too much from either of them which confirmed to me that they weren't really aware of my struggles.

Len wasn't very comfortable coming either, but he told me that he really wanted to support me and meet the psychiatrist. He told the psychiatrist that he was glad that I was seeking more conventional medicine and that I seemed to be more comfortable in my life now.

March 6 2003

My psychiatrist is giving me some more things to think about. For the last few weeks, he's been 'poking' me about right and wrong, challenging the positions I hold. I felt my anger rising. I thought he didn't care about any issues, accepting everyone's behaviour regardless of the damage that they caused. This was more important to me than the fact that he was challenging my ideas. His seeming lack of a moral compass really bothered me.

Then I realized he was trying to push me into my angry judging behaviour as a way of exposing and dealing with it. This is his method, to cause high emotions that can then be challenged as being unproductive. His point was that we often judge a person's behaviour as right or wrong without knowing the details or the explanation behind the acts. He pointed out that I was becoming angry with him because I judged his views, but I didn't know his story of trying to evoke a response in me. Judgment often comes under these circumstances so it is worth trying to understand a person's situation.

He also said that most people know when they're doing right or wrong but they often can't change their behaviour without support. To be continually told they are wrong just puts them on the defensive and achieves little.

Yes, it is difficult to change without support. This is so true for me, so I need to practice being more thoughtful and understanding of others. Perhaps this will help me to understand people more easily and not feel so alone.

In early August, Julia still feels very tired even though it's the holidays.

"I'm not working and I don't have a lot of anxiety, but I'm tired all day," she tells the psychiatrist.

He pauses, looks at Julia and says, "You berate yourself for your perceived failures and don't praise yourself for your successes. That can be exhausting. Also, you haven't found your pace. You don't stop when you need a break. You are not kind to yourself." He continued, "I don't feel tired during the day because I relax and don't hurry myself. And, if I have extra time to spare, I always have a good book with me so that I can enjoy the time."

Those are good ideas for me to incorporate into my day, thinks Julia.

My past is such a tangled web of complex intercon-
nected parts. As I explore it, there constantly seems
to be a view or perspective that I didn't see before.
But I suppose it's normal to find hidden aspects
that have lingered. I hope the day will come when
I will feel more at peace with my past.

October 5, 2003

We have a new person in group and I feel very suspicious of him. He's very set in his ways and is
struggling in his marriage. But I've made a pledge
to myself to do things differently, not to judge and
to listen carefully to his story. Perhaps then I will
be able to accept him more easily.

November 2003

My Mum is eighty-eight, I've booked tickets to go
over and see her this Christmas. I want the kids to
see her again and get a sense of their background.
My sister who lives near Mum, says I shouldn't go
over, especially since I plan to stay with Mum.
Mum, she says, is too fragile. I twist every way to
make arrangements that will work but my sister is
angry and upset. I cancel the flight tickets but
then I become angry and upset. I seem to have lost
a good relationship with my sister as well as a trip
with the family to England.

    I took the problem to the psychiatrist. I wanted
this resolved. He listened to me and as usual,

quietly nodded his head and told me that my sister has the responsibility for our Mum and so she has the authority. I felt a little better but it didn't settle things for me. I wrote a letter to my sister and took it to him to see if he thought it would help. He read it and shook his head but didn't offer any suggestions. I then took the problem to group. I got empathy but no solutions. I'm stuck. This went on for a number of weeks.

Then I found out Karen is practicing again. I booked a session through my work.

"Welcome back," says Karen "How are you doing?"

Julia responds "Karen I've come to see you with a problem. I'm now seeing a psychiatrist, but he doesn't seem to be able to help me with this problem. I thought you could give me some insight." She then goes on to explain the situation.

"So, tell me, why did you want to go over to England this Christmas?" asks Karen.

Julia has to stop and think. "I guess it was because I wanted the kids to have more of a relationship with their grandmother, and a sense of family. They haven't been to England for a while."

Karen looks pensive before answering. "I don't think its realistic for them to develop a relationship with just one visit. You might have been disappointed if you'd gone."

This helped Julia feel much better right away. "And what about the relationship with my sister?"

"Well I think that has to be done face to face. It needs to be a two-way exchange. A phone call or a letter just won't do it. You'll have to wait for that opportunity."

Julia is relieved. She has an understanding now. She feels much better.

When Julia gets home she thinks of returning to Karen for therapy, but it's expensive, there will be no group and Karen can't write prescriptions or doctor's notes. Even so, she appreciates that in one session, Karen gave her more help than the psychiatrist did in a number of sessions.

It all happened so quickly, my Mum had a fall, was taken in to hospital where she had a stroke and died. I need to go over to England for the funeral and I hope I will get a chance to make peace with my sister. I am so grateful that I saw Karen last month.

It's eight thirty on the Friday evening and Julia is sitting at the airport waiting to board the plane. This feels unreal, she thinks. I had such a strong desire to visit at Christmas, it's almost as if I had a premonition that time was running out. She feels sad and drained.

The next morning, she arrives in London early and decides to go and have a good English breakfast. However, when the food is in front of her she doesn't feel hungry and doesn't eat much. She has to wait for her middle sister and husband, who are flying in from the States and arriving later in the morning. They have rented a car, so she goes to check out where to go to pick it up.

Later in the morning they arrive. There are hugs all round, and they each check in with each other, "How are you doing?" It's not till they arrive at their mother's house after a couple of hours driving, that the reality of the loss hits them. The house is horribly empty. They hug again and cry a little. But soon there is so much to do that their grief is pushed aside. Also, making peace with her eldest sister is weighing on Julia's mind.

A few days later the three of them are standing in their eldest sister's kitchen, talking about the arrangements for the funeral.

Julia knows it's now or never. She starts with, "I hope our disagreement at Christmas isn't going to come between us. I would hate that."

"Don't be so silly! You are my sister. I love you." And they hug.

Julia is so relieved. So few words to put things in their place. Later she realizes this is the first time anyone from her family of origin has ever said, "I love you" to her.

It's a busy week making the arrangements for the funeral on Friday. The world is out of sync for Julia, as a teacher she is never free from teaching in February. It's as if she is living in two different worlds. She is very glad her sisters are willing for her to speak at the funeral as she wants to thank her Mum for supporting her. She asks everyone who is coming to the funeral for short stories about her mother and tries to incorporate them into her brief talk. The one that she remembers the most is the story of her Mum, as a little girl, loving elephants. Her Mum had a furry stuffed toy elephant. Then as a special treat she was taken to a zoo to see a real elephant. She was upset that the elephant in the zoo had lost its fur. When she was told "Elephants don't have fur!" she was angry. She took her toy elephant and cut off all the fur.

For a week Julia is immersed in this surreal world but on Saturday, February 21, she flies back to reality. Len picks her up at the airport but he has to leave the next day on business. "Will you be okay?" he asks.

"Yes, yes," she says but she really wants him to stay. The next day when she is alone, the grief hits her and she howls with tears. In a number of ways, she feels abandoned. But, she thinks, I'm glad I'm going back to work tomorrow, it'll distract me.

When she sees the psychiatrist at the end of the week, he asks, "Do you want me to write you a sick note so you have time to grieve?"

"No thanks," she says. His question underscores the disconnect she feels with him. Time off work is the last thing that she wants; she wouldn't know what to do with herself. She's sure that working will be far better for her.

April 7, 2004

I seem to be stuck. I've figured out a lot of things; I go to group, listen carefully and respond truthfully. I have improved but I still have anxiety about sleep and can easily be tipped back into an over-reaction. I need to move on but it just isn't happening. Also, I am becoming frustrated with my psychiatrist again. I want more, not just the meaningless conversations we seem to have. He doesn't seem to hear me when I tell him things. It's so difficult trying to find the best way to move forward on my own. I feel that I've got tangled thorns stuck in me and that he won't help me to pull them out. Perhaps I can just continue in group and not see him for a while.

April 20, 2004

The psychiatrist hasn't said anything to me about not making appointments with him, so I guess it's okay.

April 30, 2004

In group this week Andrea said that physical problems sometimes have a psychological origin. When we are stressed, the body starts 'whispering' to us with little complaints. Yes, I remembered that sore leg that I'd had before I stopped sleeping, the skin rashes and the irritable bowel syndrome. The body is pretty smart. So I'm trying to honour my intuition and make good choices for my life. My logical planning, organizing, thinking, and analyzing

155

mind is great for some problems but it does crowd out the nuances of my instinctive thoughts.

May 10, 2004

I'm beginning to change the dialogue, to look at some of the good things from my childhood. Although I grew up to be emotionally immature, my parents did love me. I did get a university education, which has opened up so many doors for me. I've continued and have enjoyed learning all my life. I am very persistent and do not give up easily. I am able to entertain myself and can be very creative. I am very empathetic towards others in trouble, especially animals. I am passionate about making the world a better place. Positive re-enforcement like this is so much better than dwelling on the past.

1957

It's Sunday and Dad is still asleep. But he'll be awake
by lunch time. She feels excitement and anticipation.
Some Sundays he brings sweets for them to share.
She especially likes the Fry's chocolate cream. But
sometimes it's an assortment of sweets, mostly chewy
ones that they can count out between them.

I am getting so much better. We saw the movie 'A
Beautiful Mind' last week. The image that sticks
with me is the horrible mess in the main character's office. Every inch of the walls covered with
scribbles, diagrams and scraps of paper. Information on top of information. That's how my mind
was about three years ago when I was so obsessive.
Such a mess, no clear thread, so much spiraling
around and tatters of information repeated and repeating going nowhere. All of it impinging on clear
thought. Some of this has been cleared out now, but
there's more work to do. At least I have a feeling of
the direction in which to go.

June 15, 2004

In group, Barry has been niggling at me with
lots of little jokes about my behaviour that I don't
find funny. Actually, his comments are hurtful. I
need to speak out in group. I carefully thought
about how I would do this and at the next group
told him that his jokes at my expense had to stop. It
didn't go over well and I had to think carefully
about why my approach caused such a bad reaction. I didn't understand it, this was group after
all. It goes right back to Karen telling me to address
problems with people and it was obvious that for
all my work I hadn't got any better at this. Then
with the responses from the group I realized that it
sounded as if I was telling him off, instead of telling him how hurtful it was for me because I felt

belittled by all his comments. With this kind of approach, we could have discussed the problem.

It is still so hard for me to figure out how to express myself effectively when something is wrong, but I'm getting there. At least now I do try to speak out. So often in my past, I have had the feeling that something was wrong but then argued against that feeling and ignored the situation and myself.

July 2, 2004

It came up in group this week, that women are better with language and communication and men better with science and math. I told the group how marginalized I felt by such statements and how I felt that this attitude was discriminatory. As a woman, who thinks logically and loves science and math, there is often the suggestion that I'm an oddity. It's frustrating when a man will assume that I couldn't possibly be interested in finance and talks down to me as he explains things.

Thankfully this attitude is slowly changing, but rarely in a conversation will a man ask a women her opinion on the topic. Of course, women have to stand up for themselves more and engage in meaningful conversations, but we are so cultured not to do this. Little girls are taught to listen instead of do, while little boys are encouraged to be engaged in all kinds of activities. Toys are specifically marketed to encourage the little girls to be the care-givers and the little boys to be those that interact with the world. Just look at those Saturday morning toy advertisements which never validate the little girls that like to play with trucks, or the little boys that like to play with dolls. Parents need to encourage their girls to have a range of toys including building toys and their boys to have dolls and play houses, as well as the other 'male' toys. Yes, there would still be differences between men and women but it wouldn't be so prescribed by society.

Also, I think the statement 'boys will be boys' does children such a dis-service. Boys are allowed to behave unreasonably and are not expected to control their exuberant behaviour, while girls are expected to be prim and proper and are not encouraged to be loud and noisy.

We also have to accept that women have the right to earn equal salaries to men. But in the past so many companies have claimed that they can't afford to do this. There are so many inventive ways in which this could be achieved but often women still receive less pay than men do, even when they have equal qualifications. Women are also less likely to be promoted because women are often not considered able to be leaders even though they can be very effective. There are so many examples of strong female leaders around the world.

Meanwhile the patriarchal society has given men many rights and privileges. The right to be able to do and say what they want and to expect everybody to respect their views; the right to be able to take the lead; play hardball without being considered pushy or aggressive and the right not to apologize and not to have to explain their views. We must not continue to brainwash our young women to have a subservient role in society. We need to free women around the world, they have such a great contribution to make.

Finally, North American society, has to learn not to objectify women so that their worth is solely dependent on their looks, their hairstyle, their clothes etc. But then of course the beauty corporations put their best efforts towards perpetuating this myth in the support of their profits.

Yes, I'm passionate about this and I feel it is part of my legacy to try to make changes for future generations. But I cannot do it all. I am part of a generation that was trying to prove that women were equal to men in the work force, as well as able to raise a family. I put a lot of pressure on myself to be good at both working and mothering. This, in its self, added to the unrealistic demands that I put on myself and was partly responsible for the fall into anxiety. Raising children and keeping house needs to be shared responsibilities, we need creative solutions. Men could become more involved in raising their children if more places of work offered day care and if paternity leave was better supported.

At least now I can speak about women's rights a little more calmly without becoming angry or feeling threatened.

June 18, 2004

I am slowly finding my balance. I'm getting better at listening to myself, knowing when things feel wrong and then taking steps to change them. It's taken me a long, long time, over six years, to grieve for the past so that it no longer hurts and to work on ingrained behaviours that need changing. Perhaps this has to do with the fact that I'm older—I have to overcome all those years of living with faulty guidelines. Perhaps too, I got stuck in the child's emotional state. It's true that I'm still seeking validation. But I hope I've grown up and am more like an adult now.

Its undeniable that these changes are helping me towards a better life. I'm still not quite over the anxiety about sleep, it's almost as if it's become a part of me that defies any logic. But I can see lots more understanding in my journal. It's gone from a factual list to a much more sophisticated expression of my emotions. It often contains solution to my problems. I'm wondering when the psychiatrist will tell me I'm recovered enough to leave therapy.

For those suffering
from anxiety

It's often true that people get stuck in their recovery from mental illness. Sometimes, it's because the body has reached a new norm and needs time to consolidate the progress. Sometimes, as a person begins to feel better, they are in less distress and have less of a need to move forward. Sometimes it is because they need to move on but don't know how.

Julia was stuck with the psychiatrist. She wanted a continuity from one session to the next and she wanted directives on how she could move forward. She began to mistrust him.

Chapter 9

Mistakes

July 1 2004

Things are going well for me. I'm improving, I'm changing. I can feel it in my bones. I think it's time to move forward and come off the antidepressants. I think I've changed enough in my thought patterns. I'm so much more positive. I'll reduce the dose really slowly and see where it takes me.

August 15 2004

I've been off the medication for about a month now. I feel a sense of freedom, a sense of accomplishment. I can be myself again.

September 11 2004

I have to admit it, my positive thinking is changing. I don't feel as secure that things will work out well and I'm questioning if I should have stopped the antidepressant. I feel vulnerable and have that old desire to complete everything even when I'm tired. Maybe I just need a little more time without the antidepressant to adjust. I'm a little more anxious at times but I have the sleeping pills to take if I need them.

October 4 2004

My poor mind just doesn't want to seem to stop. It's squashing me down so that I have no spontaneity. I can't hang on to the changes that I made in my behaviour. I'm exhausted, I'm sad, I'm anxious, I'm just not coping. I know the solution but I don't like to admit it. I need to start taking the antidepressants again even though I feel that I've done all the work and shouldn't need the pills.

Late October, Julia is sitting in the busy doctor's office waiting. The doctor has put her back on the antidepressants, but there's a problem.

The doctor comes in and asks, "How are you today?"

"The antidepressants seem to be giving me a sore stomach." She is not sure that the doctor will take her seriously. She fears the doctor might think she is just being oversensitive.

The doctor looks at the dejected Julia. "That's not a problem," she says in an upbeat way. "We'll put you on a stomach protector and if it's still a problem, we can change your antidepressant"

Oh! There's a solution! thinks Julia. She is relieved. This doctor never makes her feel ashamed.

Over the next few months, Julia's life starts to feel better again. She does have to change her antidepressant and she is nervous about this, but her doctor reassures her that this new antidepressant medication is good for anxiety. She still wants to stay on the lowest dose of antidepressant possible. Perhaps it's my background again, she thinks with a sigh. It was never the norm, in Julia's family of origin, to take pills. And, she remembered all those childhood dentist's visits without freezing. It caused her to avoid the dentist for years after she left home.

November 16, 2004

Why did I have trouble coming off the antidepressant? I guess those new pathways of thinking, that I'd built up in the brain, weren't strong enough or deep enough. When I came off the antidepressant my brain reverted to old ways of thinking. But thankfully I feel fine now except for my usual tiredness.

November 30, 2004

In group this week Jeanette was distraught, she talked about her sleeping pills no longer working. She'd been taking them nightly for a number of years. Now she found that even if she doubled or tripled the dose, they didn't work for her. I could feel my anxiety rising. What if the sleeping pills stopped working for me? I am so glad that I take them infrequently. But even so, I'm going to find out if there are any alternatives.

January 15, 2005

I have the opportunity to retire early this June. I think that would be a good fit for me. I still struggle with anxiety about sleep and I'm so tired all the time.

February 18, 2005

I've just found a workbook about Cognitive Behaviour Training. ('Mind over Mood – Change How You Feel and How You Think' by Greenberger and

Padesky.) I wish I had discovered this before. It has lots and lots of real practical information on how to change your thought patterns and hence your anxiety. I've been trying to get rid of this sleep anxiety for years now, but it just hasn't happened. Could this help?

Anxiety about sleep seems to be a part of my thought patterns now. So this book is great. The idea is to recognize thoughts that cause anxiety, then counter them with more realistic positive statements and to write it all down so you can see it. I've been working really hard at this. It's great to have a workbook with exercises that guide me. Sometimes though, I find that the exercises spiral me down into anxiety further as I don't believe the positive statements. I wish I had someone to help me with this.

It reminds me of the time when I tried hypnosis. I just seemed to have such a strong analytical mind that I couldn't let go and be hypnotized. Still, I do remember the hypnotist repeating the phrase, "It doesn't matter if you don't sleep." which has been very useful to me at times.

April 2005

I've decided I shall retire. I know I shall miss the teaching, I have so many positive memories. But I am so tired of struggling with sleep. This will be good for me.

2004

She's walking down the school corridor when she recognizes two kids—good kids, usually. They are both angry and pushing each other, perhaps about to fight. Instinctively she steps between them, despite the fact that they are taller than her. She puts a hand up to each. She can feel their hearts racing. She leads them into an empty classroom hoping to mediate in a positive way. She takes her time, talks to them and listens to their grievances. She knows that she has a better understanding of how to do this, because she has worked through her own problems. She offers them the solution of ignoring each other for the rest of the school year, which is only a few months. They both are willing to agree. She won't report this to the office yet and she hopes there will be no more problems. She feels good that she was able to deescalate the situation and get the kids talking a little. They have a better understanding of each other now. She feels that she has a more secure footing in the world, that her decisions have merit.

June 30, 2005

It's done! After all the goodbye speeches and presentations, I'm retired. I'm sad, I'm glad, I'm exhausted. I'm going to sleep for a month. Things are going to be a lot less stressful for me. I'm going to continue to go to group as a support. I just don't feel ready to leave the protection of the psychiatrist's practice.

January 2006

I'm better now. I've gone over six months with very little anxiety and the occasional use of sleeping pills. I have no stressors on me, life is easy. I'm going to very slowly lower the antidepressant, I am going to be fine.

September 2006

I'm doing great, eight months without antidepressants. My world is under control. Len is retiring next March and we are planning to take a holiday to New Zealand and Australia to celebrate both of our retirements. I'm really looking forward to it.

October 2006

My dream trip isn't my dream trip any more, I'm becoming so desperately anxious. I can't imagine canceling the trip but I also can't imagine going on the trip. The indecision is the worst of all. I just want all of this to go away. I am so tired of all my reactions overwhelming me. I want to escape by never having to make another decision, but I know this isn't escaping. It's locking me in, controlling my world so that it becomes unbearably small.

When I calm down and think positively, I convince myself that I can do this trip, but there are things about it that really scare me. What will I do if I don't sleep? This spinning around isn't healthy. I can deal with some fears by pushing through them and doing the things that frighten me. But my fear of not sleeping—I can't control sleep, it's a different matter. I become frozen and stuck unable to cross this bridge of fear. I know this bridge so well but I can't cross it on my own, I need help. I've decided to take this to group to get support and help.

October 16, 2006

Group was terrible. They just didn't get it. How could I be anxious about a dream trip? I felt alienated and upset by them. There are many different people in group since I first started, perhaps they don't really know me, know my anguish about sleep.

October 20, 2006

I'm seeing the psychiatrist again but added to my distress we disagree.

He looked at Julia and sighed, "You know, it doesn't matter whether you go on this trip or not."

"But I want to, for me and my husband, I'm just so scared"

"Julia, you are always trying to be that eagle instead of a seagull. It's okay to be the seagull."

Oh, thinks Julia, *he's used that statement on me before. I hate it, it diminishes me, it just parallels what I was taught as a girl. "You can never have the opportunities open to a boy." I want to be the eagle, I can be the eagle. Doesn't he get it? Why can't he just help me with the anxiety? I just wish I could see Karen but I don't have access to her because I'm retired.*

October 22 2006

I feel hurt and abandoned. I find myself writing him letters about how his therapy is not helping me. I choose one to leave at the office.

October 24 2006

I'm shaken to my core. He tells group that I have written him a letter that has made him angrier than he's ever been. There's a stunned silence in the group. Somehow, I feel he's crossed a boundary. This was a private letter to him with things I hoped would open up a dialogue with him. Shouldn't he have asked my permission before sharing this information with the group. How does this help me? After he had spoken, I immediately thought, I have to show him I'm mature enough to take this and listen to what he has to say. But now the whole thing doesn't sit right with me.

November 10 2006

I've had extra sessions with him, together with his partner Andrea. At the most recent session, she asks me how I would feel if I wasn't going on the trip, I tell her the anxiety would go away. She suggests I could keep this relaxed feeling with me and still go on the trip. I feel better. I like her. Then in that moment I think, I've got to tell it, I may never get a chance again.

1959

One of the lodgers said he would take her swimming, at the local pool. She's excited, she loves swimming. He invites her up to his room in the attic to make plans. They are talking, he hangs out his penis and asks her if she knows what it is. She's frozen. He says all she's got to do is show him what she has "down there" and he'll take her swimming. She so wants to go swimming, he's been kind to her, so she tentatively lowers her pants. He lunges toward her but she can move faster than he can and she's gone, gone, gone, out the door, down the stairs, away from the attic with her heart hammering. She's so disappointed and frightened but she has no one to tell. She feels so ashamed of herself.

The psychiatrist mutters, "I didn't know."

Julia counters, "You never asked." She's angry with him for never asking more questions about her past, not providing a safe space for her to tell. After all she's been coming here for a lot of years. However, Julia feels lighter—not of the anxiety it's still there, but this secret had been weighing her down so heavily. It's the last piece of her past that she had to tell.

Andrea asks her, "How do you think this has affected your sexuality?"

Before she gets a chance to answer he interrupts, "You are so anxious about this trip that I suggest you cancel it. I have an anxious patient who went on a trip and ended up in a foreign hospital. That would not be good for you."

He has given her advice as to what to do, but there is no follow up to the disclosure that she has just made.

November 24, 2006

I'm not going to see the psychiatrist any more, he is dragging me down even further. It seems to be a usual pattern of mine, to persist at things that are not working for me. This is a difficult decision; it feels as if I am abandoning my safety net. But deep down I know it is the right decision for all concerned. I should have made it way earlier. All the signs were there.

November 30, 2006

My husband has canceled the holiday. That was a great relief; I expected the anxiety would go away now. But it doesn't. My usual pattern. Once I'm in anxiety it takes a lot to relieve it. I'm horribly disappointed in myself. I don't think I'll ever sleep again. Sleeping pills give me only a little relief. I seem to have become anxious about anxiety, afraid that it will not go away. One day as I'm sitting there feeling scared and trying to cope, my heart starts to beat really fast. But I've read about this, these panic attacks. I actually laugh at myself and say "Don't even begin to think that you can go there and do that to me." The heart beat slows. So if I can stop a panic attack why can't I stop anxiety?

December 6, 2006

I'm not calming down, I'm still in that terrible spinning anxiety. The patterns are there, I have to start taking antidepressants again even though I was fine without them for quite a while. I've made an appointment to see the doctor. I'm taking steps to help myself.

December 15, 2006

My doctor has been wonderfully supportive. She hasn't scolded me for coming off the antidepressants again.

She sees my pain and listens. She said "Anxiety usually comes back to bite you in the tail." Two weeks in and I'm still anxious. She has increased my dose. I've lost a great deal over this, it's traumatizing me. I'm so sad about this.

January 2007

And I'm still anxious. The doctor increased the dose again and told me that perhaps it would be another two weeks before the antidepressant worked. I was devastated. How can I live like this for another two weeks. I can't sleep, I have no appetite and I can't concentrate on anything. I have to accept that I'm ill. I have an anxiety disorder and probably will have to take the pills for the rest of my life.

I visited a friend to talk this over as I'm beginning to feel that the antidepressants will never work for me. He said hang in there until the pills work. Then he distracted me from my obsession as much as he could. The visit encouraged me to believe that the pills would work. Acceptance of how ill I am is difficult.

The shakes of anxiety are abating. I can go out and feel almost normal although I am constantly distracted by thoughts of not sleeping. I've been in an awful place for about six weeks. I really did believe that I wouldn't ever get well again. It was hell. That's the trouble with anxiety, it seems impossible to overcome when you are in it. I NEVER want to go there again. My doctor says she will never forget the expression on my face when she told me the pills might take another two weeks to work. But thanks to her and my friends' help I have a chance to get better. I fear things more than most people. The medicine helps so much but now I am on a higher dose. Perhaps I will always be hung up about sleep. This has been a tough lesson. I really thought I was over all this.

February 2007

I am so tired. And so sad. I feel I'm constantly walking a tight rope and if I'm not careful I'll fall off it into anxiety. I'm scared of over commitments and I'm unsure of where to go from here. At least the anxiety has abated and I feel a little more normal in my thinking. I'm trying to appreciate what I have.

I have to feel proud, that in this difficult time of anxiety, I put myself first and walked away from a psychiatrist who was not helping me. But, I have to admit I re-traumatized myself by stopping the antidepressants.

Setbacks are common, though, in this kind of journey. The new pathways of thinking had sustained me for a while but those old pathways of anxiety slowly became reinforced when I came off the antidepressants.

Obviously the upcoming travel of the dream holiday was a trigger for me and caused the old pathways of anxiety to open up. This anxiety was terrible, I think it reinforced the old pathways making them more deeply ingrained. I was in a high level of anxiety and was in deathly fear. So now I'm on a higher dose of medication. Perhaps, those first years, I wasn't taking a high enough dose of antidepressants because I still felt anxious about sleep. So this higher dose is what I really need.

March 14, 2007

I've had a little time to think about how I became stuck in therapy with the psychiatrist. Right from the beginning and a number of times after, I felt suspicious of his actions and I don't think I ever really lost that feeling. Because of the suspicion, I unknowingly kept a part of myself closed off to him. I remember when he asked why I wore so many rings. I was embarrassed to say that I felt it made me seem younger and more interesting. I didn't want to appear silly or frivolous, so I just shrugged my shoulders. He didn't really have a chance to get to know me and I don't think he understood how reticent English people are to speak about themselves.

Perhaps I could have recovered more quickly if I'd moved onto another therapist or back to Karen. I have to forgive myself for staying, when my intuition told me that things were not working. In some ways, I was using him as an access to the group that I really liked. But now I know I stayed too long there too.

The more I think about it, the more I can see fundamental differences between the way he practiced therapy and the way Karen practiced. And, I have to admit I had a close bond with Karen because she was the first person that I trusted with the story of my abusive background.

Karen gathered information from me, took careful notes, then gave her ideas to me with suggestions of activities to think about and things to work through. There was continuity from one session to the next as Karen referred to her notes and asked incisive follow up questions. As I answered these, I developed a better understanding of myself. Karen listened to my stories and showed empathy, especially when I was upset. It was empowering for me to feel validated for one of the first times in my life. Karen also checked periodically that I felt the therapy was being effective. So this was the kind of help that I expected and wanted from the psychiatrist.

But this didn't happen. The psychiatrist, of course, had his own distinctive style. The group was an important part of his practice because each week he could follow up with his patients

180

individually to discuss and maybe question their reactions from group. And he did see his patients each week. Whenever he did challenge me and push me about my reactions, it was very effective. It would give me a sudden flash of insight that shifted my thinking. Certainly experiencing a resolution, when being challenged, is emotionally very powerful. But this didn't happen often because I was too busy making sure I gave the 'right' feedback instead of saying how I really felt. And I was too good at 'being British'—guarding my own feelings—to allow him to push me into confrontation about an issue.

Both modes of treatment are very valid. But for me, Karen was a better fit. She acted like a loving parent, by appealing to my logic when she asked follow-up questions or gave me advice. It all comes down to be able to finding the 'right' therapist—a difficult thing for a vulnerable person. There's no doubt that the psychiatrist helped me a lot but he also caused me distress.

March 24, 2007

I am still exhausted and my doctor has referred me to a chronic fatigue doctor in the city. It seems that this syndrome is now being more widely accepted in the medical community. I will have to wait to see her, but it is a step forward.

For those suffering
from anxiety

If you are in therapy, consider if the therapist is right for you. Karen reached Julia's deep inner self, but this was not true of the psychiatrist. Julia knew this from an early stage in her treatment with him. She needed to look for options and she needed to have the courage to leave. But she was a vulnerable and anxious person. She felt more comfortable staying with what she knew, instead of moving on to the unknown. There is an important lesson here; to persist at something that is not working has no benefits and can even be harmful.

Don't do as Julia did and come off antidepressants without medical supervision. It can cause a lot of anguish and result in the need for a higher dose of medication. Some people can leave the medications behind but this was not the case for Julia.

Do look at Cognitive Behaviour Training. It can be very valuable early in your recovery. It has been mentioned as a useful tool at the end of Chapter Six.

Chapter 10

Healing at last

April 30 2007

I have a new therapist, Rita.

Julia rings the doorbell of another front door. *Here I am again,* she thinks nervously. *I hope this will work out, that she will be a good fit for me.*

A younger woman opens the door. "Hello. Welcome. Are you Julia? Come in."

Julia nods her head, enters and slips off her shoes.

"I'm Rita, come on downstairs with me."

Julia enters the large basement room and sees a couch and a large, comfy swivel chair in the corner. In the centre of the room, about hip height is what looks like a sand box. But Julia's eyes are drawn to all the shelves surrounding the room. There are shelves and shelves of little figurines: people, animals, houses, plants and mythical creatures some of which are covered with glitter. It looks almost magical.

"This is my work space. Sometimes I have my clients use the figurines to build a sand plate. This is especially therapeutic for children but it helps adults too. Still, come and sit down and be comfortable."

Julia already likes Rita, likes the surroundings. She sits on the couch and Rita folds herself into the chair with a notebook on her lap.

May 7, 2007

I think Rita will work well for me as a therapist
and I loved her office. I feel safe there. She's empathetic and listens. Telling her my background story
today was almost boring. I think that's good—it
means it's past stuff and no longer has an emotional hold on me. She is very supportive and
talks to me about my anxiety and sleep. She says
they are old fears and she will try to help me put
them behind me. My relationship with her seems
to be more on an adult-to-adult footing. I've grown
up over these years of therapy.

June 10, 2007

Rita did an exercise with me of imagining a visit
with my little girl self. Of course, it was a mind
exercise, but I could clearly see this little girl tentatively checking out her world to see where she fit
in. A shy little thing, but when this cautious little
girl was given a chance, she had lots to say. She
was bursting to share her world with someone, she
wanted a friend so she could talk about all the
things that mattered to her. The message is, 'I need
to nurture all these things in me'.

July and August 2007

Rita asked me to imagine a place, in that old
house of my childhood, where I was frightened. I
could see it so clearly. There was a dark passage-
way from the kitchen to the servant's old sitting
room, now the boot room. This passage-way then

185

led round the corner past the pantry to a gaping dark hole of the cellar. I'd often be sent to the pantry to get something for Mum. I hated it—the lighting was so poor. I was so scared of the opening to the cellar and didn't like the large cold dim pantry with only one little window, high up. I can still hear the sound of the latch on the pantry door and feel my heart racing.

So my homework was to redraw that area so that it no longer frightened me. That was easy, I could do that. Lots of light and a pretty door with glitter on it. Then the cellar would be closed off—along with anything that was in there. In Rita's follow up she said, "Now imagine taking each of your fears and re-framing it this way so it doesn't frighten you." I get it. I understand where she is coming from.

September 2007

I've gotten an appointment to see the chronic fatigue specialist. I feel excited. This could really help.

In October, Julia goes to the specialist's appointment.

After the introductions the specialist says, "Chronic fatigue is difficult to diagnose but I see you had a viral infection at the end of 1999 into 2000 and that you kept complaining of tiredness for which your doctor could find no physical cause. This sounds as if it could well be the beginning of chronic fatigue. I'm going to send you for several blood tests just to be sure that there isn't any other cause."

Julia nods.

"I see from the check list you've filled out that you are not refreshed by sleep; you have post exertion fatigue the following day after exercise; you have muscle aches and pains, swollen lymph nodes, low blood pressure, dizziness, swollen ankles, cold extremities and sensitivity to chemicals and foods that often result in skin rashes and diarrhea. Quite a list, but all indications of chronic fatigue. We need to get you well."

"Is that possible?" asks Julia. "I heard there is no cure to chronic fatigue."

"There's no pill that you can take, but there is lots we can do. For the next month I want you to fill out a daily log of all of your activities so we can see what's going on. I want you to pace yourself, rest often and take regular breaks in the day. Do less—way less—and have an afternoon nap if you feel tired. Your body is exhausted. It needs time to heal."

Julia starts her daily log and goes to the lab for the blood tests.

"Wow, these are a lot of tests," says the technician. "I want you to lie down for this." Twenty vials later the technician pulls out the needle and asks her to hold the cotton wool on the small needle hole. She goes out and comes back with a glass of water. "Lie here for now, I'll check you shortly."

When she comes back, she instructs Julia to stand up slowly. "How is that?" she asks. Any dizziness?"

Julia shakes her head. "No."

The technician nods. "Okay then. You're good to go, as long as there's no dizziness."

In November, Julia returns to the specialist.

She tells her, "All your tests are fine except your thyroid is on the low side. I'm going to prescribe a very low dose of synthroid for that. You may have more energy once you start it."

Julia feels incredible relief. "So there is a cause for my tiredness?"

"Low thyroid doesn't account for all your tiredness and symptoms but, certainly for some of it. Let's have a look at your daily log. Mmm, this is pretty good, you are taking lots of breaks."

"Yes. But it's so difficult to do so little. I feel I'm wasting time."

"Try and think of it, not as time wasted, but as time getting well. I see here that anxiety has been a very bad problem for you. This could be the cause of your chronic fatigue because anxiety exhausts your body. It depletes your adrenaline and cortisol. I'm recommending a programme out of England on chronic fatigue run by Ashok Gupta. It comes as a series of DVD's and is called 'Amygdala Re-training.' You can google it. It costs about two hundred dollars but it is well worth it. In the meantime, keep taking those breaks and rests during the day and I'll see you in three months."

I feel good about this, thinks Julia. She is acknowledging my tiredness and giving me suggestions to alleviate it.

December 1, 2007

A package arrived for me today. I'm excited, it's the Gupta Amygdala Re-training programme. There's a big chart to put on the floor, a work book and at least ten DVD's as well as a CD with three guided meditations.

December 15, 2007

The introductory DVDs are great. They explain what's happening in the brain with chronic fatigue and Gupta talks of anxiety about anxiety. No-one has understood this before when I tried to tell them. Gupta explains that the amygdala is a part of the brain that responds to emotion. In anxiety, the amygdala gets stimulated to protect you from the dangers around. That's the normal process of survival. But if the anxiety continues, then the amygdala gets over stimulated, goes into overdrive and alerts your body to every little thing around you. This causes all those sensitivities and the fatigue. This so fits the biology that I know and the symptoms that I've been having. I feel so hopeful.

January 3, 2008

According to Gupta, the amygdala is a primitive part of the brain and doesn't respond to logical thought, you can't just tell it to stop over-reacting. But Gupta maintains that if you talk out loud frequently enough with the same message then over a number of months you can 'retrain your amygdala', calm it down and this in turn will calm down the anxiety. It sounds a bit hokey but it's worth a try. What have I got to lose?

February 15, 2008

This talking to myself out loud, as if I was giving advice, seems to be helping me. Over the years, I self-counseled by saying in my mind, "You need this" or "You need that", "You have a problem of over-reacting but you can change your behaviour". Even some of my journals were written using 'You' so I could give advice to myself. So I was familiar with addressing myself in this way. But I'd never spoken any of this out loud.

February 20, 2008

We're going to go on a cruise, my favourite type of traveling. I can feel myself getting a little anxious about being able to sleep but I'm using the Gupta technique to interrupt those thoughts and calm myself. To add to that I am on an antidepressant.

March 1, 2008

Yes, I do feel anxious about the trip but I went six weeks without sleeping and I was okay. This trip is only a week. It'll be fine.

When I visited Rita this week, I was feeling somewhat anxious. She said, "Look around the room. What is there here to cause you anxiety?" I could instantly see that it was useless to be anxious in that moment.

March 17, 2008

I feel great. We had such a good time on the trip. I took sleeping pills for the first few days and then things fell into place. I hope trips will continue to be easier like this. I don't want my fear of not sleeping to limit my travel.

April 18, 2008

Each moment I am calm, I am grateful. Even when I'm tired, life has so much to offer me. I'm continuing to work on the Gupta programme for chronic fatigue. It's going to take months to work through all the CDs.

June 20, 2008

As I'm going through the programme, lots of exercises are coming up that I've done before but its a refresher course, a reminder of the underlying things that can cause anxiety.

Meanwhile I'm continuing to talk out loud to myself when I have negative thoughts especially about sleep. It helps. It makes me feel calmer and then I find I'm less bothered by the thoughts in subsequent days.

I've started a huge chart in the bedroom with phrases that inspire me and help me to feel better. This technique seems to be working for me. I've started to tell my anxiety to go away, tell it that it's not based in reality, and that things will be fine. I'm actually beginning to believe this, a new concept for me.

August 2008

Rita is a good support for me. I've talked to her about the Gupta technique, she's interested and is encouraging me. So much seems to just have fallen into place. I'm gaining a rush of confidence, it feels great. I've just got to remind myself not to put myself down.

Rita has also helped me with my relationship with my husband. Helping him to see that some of my behaviours, with which he becomes exasper-ated, are a result of my background. He's become more empathetic when I over react or become upset. She also helped me to see how I could be more sup-portive of him.

September 2008

Rita suggested, this session, that I try to put myself into anxiety, think the thoughts that put me there. I've lived with anxiety so long that I thought it would be easy, but I couldn't put myself there. She said that if I can't put myself into that familiar place of the past, that signals an improvement. She also reminded me that when I feel anxious to look around me to see if there is anything actually there to threaten me. To take the fear out of my head.

December 2008

Rita keeps encouraging me. She says I am so much more confident and have changed a lot of the old behaviours that have given me angst. She says my fear about sleep is 'old stuff', not relevant to me anymore.

January 2009

Rita suggested it's time to face the fears around sleep. "When your body is tired enough it will sleep. You are not working. You have no commitments." She suggested that for one week I put the sleeping pills away, go to bed and see what happens. Also, if I don't sleep within an hour to get up and do something. This seems tough to me, as I know from experience that without sleep I tend to go into anxiety. But she encouraged me by telling me that this old anxiety was no longer relevant to me.

February 2009

We are painting a room. I could try this sleep exercise of Rita's and if I don't sleep get up and paint.

February 2009

The first night, after tossing and turning, I got up about half an hour after midnight and did some painting until I was very tired. That night I went to sleep at about six in the morning. I repeated this for the next two nights and went to sleep at four in the morning and then two in the morning respectively. I then fell into a reasonable pattern of night sleeping. I feel emotionally so much stronger now. I have faced my fear and nothing terrible happened.

February 2009

Rita was delighted for me that I'd made it. "You were just ready," she said, as she clapped her hands. I know the pattern of sometimes not sleeping, isn't going to vanish instantly, but at least I can accept it and not go into anxiety. I can logically tell myself that it doesn't matter if I don't sleep and believe it because I proved it to myself. I have accepted that sleeplessness is okay, just as I did years ago when my father died. But at that time I couldn't sustain the feeling. Now I can. This is the cure for me, the cure that my second therapist Anna tried to get me to accept about eight years back. I guess I just wasn't in the right place at the time to hear her and be able to move forward. Just think, if I'd been able to work on this with her, so much could have been avoided.

March 2009

According to Rita, people that have had an abusive background as children are much more careful and distrustful, much more fearful of ordinary situations, than people who don't have this background. She tells me that a video of walking through a dark forest can evoke completely different emotions in abused and non-abused people. Add a little tense music and the abused person can become very agitated. So, she is helping me to recognize certain reactions as belonging in the past, that they no longer have relevance in my life. It is a freeing way of viewing things. When I over-react I can just shrug my shoulders and say "That's old stuff", instead of berating myself for my reactions.

August 2009

I am seeing Rita a lot less frequently now but it's comforting to know that she is there if I have anything important to discuss.

I really think I'm getting there, to a place where I can feel happy and comfortable about things. I've gone over three months without using any sleeping pills. I'm doing so much more for myself now, reacting more spontaneously and developing friendships. It's time to stop trying to improve myself so relentlessly and to just be.

November 2009

I got a chance to see Karen, the therapist that started me out on this journey, just for a few sessions. It was like coming home. I mentioned that there was a sexual assault in my childhood that I'd never told her about. She immediately asked if I needed to talk about and process it. It was lovely to feel that she cared about me and it was empowering to be able to say no and mean it. I could see that as a child I had prevented myself from becoming a victim by running away, although, I do wish I had told someone. I now know that sexual predators like this learn from their mistakes and go on to effectively assault other children and cause untold damage.

Anyway, we talked about my dad a lot, and how empathetic I feel towards him now. How I feel that British society had made things difficult for him. She asked me about all the things that I wanted to tell him to make his life easier. I replied that I'd tell him how I missed having him around as a father; how I wished I had known him better; how sorry I was that society pushed him to have to prove himself; how unfair it was that he had to work so hard to establish his business and how smart he was with a great sense of humour hidden under all the stresses of 'trying to make the grade'. It was a heartrending session for me especially when Karen said "Now turn all that advice on to yourself." That was great therapy.

Thank you Karen.

Final Words

So comes the end of Julia's story, which you may have guessed is my story. She was a creation that gave me a way to dispassionately present all the things that had happened to me, to distance myself from all those underlying emotions. My British upbringing still had influence on me; it was just so much more comfortable to write about Julia than to write about myself.

In the book, I've recalled the dialogue in my therapy sessions to the best of my ability and improvised where I felt there was a need. Some of the dates of the journals are also a best guess as I didn't always record the date. But the journals and flashbacks are authentically my own truth. I so clearly remember the first flashback that I wrote. The psychiatrist asked me to write about why I liked animals so much. He explained that a veterinarian had asked him to collect information. I wanted to write something a little different. And so I wrote the 1957 "flashback" about my cat. Part of this writing was included in the story earlier, but here is the full version that I gave to him.

1957

She's sitting on her own, on an old dusty staircase, the back staircase in an old house way out in the country. There is a great depth of sadness and loneliness surrounding her. But sitting on her lap, purring is a black and white cat. The cat always has time for her especially if she's gentle and kind. It even sneaks up onto her bed at night although if it's caught it's put outside. And it always comes to sleep with her if she's sick. She feels a great sense of comfort in the presence of cat. It always accepts her exactly the way she is. It's reliable, she can trust it, its behaviour is consistent, it never lashes out unless it's provoked. But the people in this child's world are confusing, they constantly make her feel inadequate, awkward, frightened. They are always telling her what to do, but the rules keep changing, she doesn't know when things are right, when she's safe. These people can lash out unexpectedly, hurt her even though she can't figure out what's wrong.

I was proud of this little bit of writing, as for the first time, I could hear my own voice loud and clear. I was so disappointed with his response. He quietly sat in his chair, read the passage, thanked me and then pushed the paper forward onto his desk without a comment. I felt dismissed, a feeling that he often evoked in me. I'd wanted to hear what he thought and I at least expected him to acknowledge my hurtful past. His empathy would have offered me some validation of the things that I'd lost.

But that was not his style of therapy. This added to the feeling of distrust that was slowly growing. It's a pity, we just seemed to slide past each other without understanding. I just wanted to know how to deal with my anxiety so I could live a normal life; he was trying to change some of my thought patterns so I could live more comfortably in the world. The lesson—to move on if the therapy isn't working—took me a long time to learn. I gave him the benefit of the doubt too often. On the other hand, I moved on from Anna too quickly.

But, back to the flashbacks, I later found this style of writing a wonderful way of speaking my own truth and so incorporated it into the book. And I have to admit that writing this book has given me some internal validation and allowed me to forgive myself for all my missteps. A kind of therapy in its own way, as well as a celebration.

Going through my old journals, that wind round and round the same problems for years, allows me to appreciate all the anguish of my struggle. It brings me back to the words that I spoke to the organizer at that lunch, "I wish I'd taken the drugs earlier". Without the antidepressants, I experienced traumatic anxiety. This trauma then reverberated through my thinking for many years and caused me a lot of pain and suffering. With the antidepressants I would have been more relaxed and not have delved so deeply into every aspect of my past. I think I could have moved forward much more effectively with less pain and without the traumatic anxiety. Perhaps

I would have been healthy enough to have come off the antidepressants, once the psychological work was done.

On the other hand, if I had taken the antidepressants right at the beginning, I might never have dealt with those hidden feelings that needed to be addressed for me to function happily in the world. Doing this emotional work was so important for me. It allowed me to understand the causes of my anxiety. I felt less to blame, less like a broken person.

Considering my personality, background and the profession that I had chosen for my life, I think it was inevitable that I would suffer anxiety. If I'd grown up in different circumstances, anxiety would probably never have touched my life. But struggling through the anxiety has made me a stronger, more empathetic person, much more in touch with myself and others around me. And in some ways it has allowed me to grow up. I think my development was emotionally stuck in a child's world always seeking validation and always doing what others told me. I am so glad that I am no longer being held back by my baggage. I have a sense of peace and freedom without the past dragging me down. I feel more at liberty to show people who I really am, less of a need to hide myself because I feel inadequate.

If you have a story anything like mine, please know there is hope for your future. Each of us has our own journey, that will reflect our individuality and background. There is no right way of getting better.

I still wish I could come off the antidepressants, but now I know, given my history, the risk is too great. Also I think the journey is never completely over; writing this book brought lots more understanding of myself and the types of therapy that I had received, what worked for me, what didn't and why.

Following is what I think I needed when I first presented with anxiety and sleeplessness:

A sympathetic doctor who would have said, "Anxiety and sleeplessness are common in your late forties because estrogen levels are fluctuating wildly. This will eventually become easier but in the mean-time I'm going to put you on a low dose of antidepressant which will calm the anxiety. This will take about two weeks to work and will give you mild side effects such as a dry mouth, but these will go away after a few weeks. I'll also give you some sleeping pills that you can take if you need them until the antidepressant starts working. I'll see you in a couple of weeks to see how you are doing. I also strongly suggest you see a therapist in case there are some hidden psychological causes to your anxiety. And a therapist can also teach you how to manage anxious thoughts so they are not so overwhelming. There's an excellent technique called Cognitive Behaviour Therapy, it's worth investigating. I'll give you some therapists' names if you need."

But would I have listened? Probably not, given my family dialogue of only taking pills if absolutely necessary; my past clashes with doctors over natural child-birth and hormone replacement therapy and my inherent distrust of people.

It has been such a long journey. I've had lots of stumbles along the way, besides coming off the antidepressants twice without medical supervision. I grieved too long, and spent too many years examining and trying to change flawed behaviours. I got stuck half way trying too hard 'to do everything right'. I just have to look back at all the lists I made for myself of what I had to do to get better, all those grateful statements, all the letters I wrote, all the conversations I had with my young self, all that analysis of what was wrong with me. I was actually too persistent, too much of a perfectionist and didn't know when to step away.

I recognize this is a repeated pattern of my past. I had difficulty walking away from a harmful boyfriend, from hurtful 'friends', from people manipulating me and from my own persistence to do things perfectly. And most of all, I did not move on from therapy that I knew was not working, therapy that allowed me to get stuck. Eventually I had to let go and stop standing in my own way. I had to trust that my mind had the ability to work things out subconsciously. I had to face my fears and let healing happen knowing I'd done a lot of necessary work to help me on my way.

In a way, my illness was a blessing. I have learned not to be suspicious of the whole world and to have a freer mode of functioning so that I can be happier. I've confronted my fears about sleep and many other things. This has given me such a different view on life.

My writing lets me see the tenacity and courage that I had at times; reminds me of past wisdoms that are still relevant today; allows me to be a stronger and more confident person, and my writing has allowed me to put any lingering feelings of sadness into a proper perspective.

Thankfully, these days my past rarely hurts me and I have been able to challenge many of the behaviours precipitated by my hidden secrets. I have been able, for the most part to put anxiety out of my life and with it the chronic fatigue. A gluten free diet also helped as I have found out that I am gluten intolerant. I feel at peace. I have found my style, and life is so much more enjoyable. When old behaviours come up, which of course they do, I can say 'It's old stuff, it's in the past, and it doesn't matter if I don't sleep.'

My family members remind me when I'm being controlling, when I'm being pessimistic, when I'm over-reacting and when I'm hiding my real opinions again. It's so easy to slip back, but now I can recognize it and stop it from causing me, or those around me, any harm. Thankfully now, I've stopped putting little notes up all round the house to remind me of the changes that I needed to accomplish.

If the anxiety about sleep tries to raise it's ugly head, I acknowledge it, check it out for validity and maybe make necessary changes. There are still times when I don't sleep, and yes I get frustrated. I think I'll always be more sensitive about sleep than most people. But I usually don't get anxious. I have techniques that work for me. I might meditate, listen to music, get up and read or if I'm really tired and feel I must sleep, I'll take a sleeping pill. The sleeplessness always goes away, the sensitivity is just part of the older messaging that is no longer relevant to me. Mainly now, I keep the sleeping pills for when I travel, to deal with the jet lag and the hectic pace of tours.

Now my life gives me lots of joy. I write, I read, I teach a little, I garden in the good weather, I walk most days, I volunteer in the community and I travel lots. In 2019, we went on that dream vacation that got abandoned so many years ago. New Zealand and Australia are wonderful. I also visit Cambodia, where we support a village school that gives free classes in English and computers to school aged children. I even get to teach Cambodian kids English and coach the young teachers. Plus, I'm learning the language.

I have a wonderful little rescue cat who makes me smile so much. In my way, I am paying a debt owed to the cats of my youth that gave me comfort.

I will always have empathy for the underdog and am constantly writing protest letters on social issues. It helps to dispel my anger at the injustices of the world. I need to stop taking all the world's problems on my shoulders, to let up a little and only do what I can. But I still feel that someone has to do it. By being inactive we become complicit to egregious behaviour. So I encourage you to choose your issue, and support it your own way.

I say I am healed, but I know the story never really stops. As I wrote this book, I had to acknowledge that I was still trying to fulfill my needs for the validation I missed as a child. But more positively, I lost my anger against the psychiatrist and acknowledged the good things he did for me. I shall always find it difficult to expresses myself verbally, saying the wrong things at the wrong time, but despite this I do feel that I have a voice in this world.

Things could have been a lot worse. Life may not have given me the opportunity to learn about myself, to change, and to chase away the demons that inhabited my head. To live in constant anxiety is no way to exist. Life needs to be enjoyed and embraced, to give us uplifting moments that allow us to be aware of the beauty that surrounds us.

2021

It's dark and late into the night. She is woken by the gentle meowing and purping of her little cat who has just jumped onto the bed. She smiles. She's happy. She remembers the lunch today with four friends to celebrate a birthday. She had so much fun, they laughed so much. This was the first they'd eaten together in a restaurant for almost two years. The vaccinations for Covid are changing things. She feels a lot of love towards the person lying beside her even though he is snoring a little. He supported her, helped her so much through those long dark days of anxiety. It is wonderful to feel that the anxiety is in the past, to feel confident that she can face the world.

You gain strength, courage and confidence by every
experience in which you really stop
to look fear in the face ...
You must do the thing that you think you cannot.

~ Eleanor Roosevelt

Appendices

The following Appendices, have all been written by me to help the anxiety sufferer. I am not an expert, except from the point of view that I suffered through anxiety for ten years. My advice is based on that which worked for me. I hope it will be useful to you.

All of the factual information is accurate to the best of my knowledge and, I think, adds a fascinating dimension to this condition of anxiety.

$\mathcal{A}ppendix$ I

Explanation of things that may help you with anxiety:

The list on the back page gives basic suggestions of immediate things that you can do for yourself when suffering anxiety. But because each person's anxiety is different, things that work for one person may not be useful for another. You do have to find your own way to an effective treatment, sometimes a daunting task when you are in so much distress. To help with this, here are some further details concerning the points from the back page. I hope this helps you in your journey.

See your doctor

Sometimes this isn't as simple as it seems. You need to feel that you trust your doctor to do what's best for you, you need to feel heard by your doctor. This is a relationship that takes time to build. If things don't feel right, you need to tell your doctor that as part of the discussion of your treatment. If you really feel that your doctor doesn't understand and is not treating you effectively, change your doctor.

Medication

Medication can be very valuable in controlling your anxiety, but there are many different antidepressants available and some may not be effective for you. This is why it's important to describe all your symptoms to your doctor so he/she can use their skills in choosing the best medication for you. Thankfully today's antidepressants have minimal side effects and are tolerated well but it's important when you first start taking these drugs that you see your doctor regularly. Then he/she can assess the situation and decide if that drug is the best for you. (See Appendix III on antidepressants.)

See a therapist

Perhaps you or your partner's work place offers free therapy sessions. This is a great place to start as it gives you a feel for what might work for you. Your doctor is also a great resource for recommending a good therapist. Therapy can be expensive, but a few therapists are covered by government funding, although they usually have long waiting-lists. Seeing a therapist helps you to learn about yourself and to understand the causes of your anxiety. It also helps you to learn about behaviours that are perhaps damaging to you and how to make some of the necessary changes in your life that will help you to feel grounded and secure.

It is important, though, to find the right therapist for you. You must feel safe because you are going to reveal some of your innermost thoughts and feelings. A good therapist will help you to move forward in your journey within about three to six months. And they will check with you from time to time to see if the therapy is helping you and if you have any needs that are not being met by the therapy. If you feel you are stuck in your treatment and your therapist isn't listening or helping, change your therapist.

As well as individual therapy, group therapy can be a very valuable part of your treatment. It provides a sense of not being alone, that there are other people out there that suffer and struggle in a way similar to you. And these people, these 'non-experts' have so much wisdom to share and you will find that you also have wisdom to share that you can use on yourself as well.

Journal

This is a way of getting in touch with your feelings and opinions about the world around you. It gives you a chance to reveal and understand your authentic self. There is no judgment, you are free to write what you like, as it is just for you. And once the emotions are out on the page you may feel a validation of your intuition. You are no longer weighed down. And you might just find those solutions that you need. Also, over time you can see how far you have come in your recovery.

Changing behaviours that get you into emotional problems

If the therapist has helped you to identify behaviours that add to your anxiety, and that you'd like to change, you are half way there in understanding how to get better. But these changes don't come easily, especially if they've been with you for a while. It is a lot of work and takes time. You need to practice, practice, practice the new behaviour. If you are in group therapy, this is the first place to start that practice. Even so, you have to actively look for opportunities to make small changes in what you say and do when interacting with people. Maybe, be a little more assertive, a little more accepting or a little less angry depending on your problem. Each tiny step counts. Rehearse phrases that you can use in certain circumstances so you have them ready. The changes can take months or years to become a normal way of behaving and you can easily slip back into old habits. Be reflective and celebrate the slightest change as a success.

Cognitive Behaviour Training

Cognitive Behaviour Training can be a powerful tool in dealing with anxiety. It teaches anxious people to first, identify their negative thoughts and then to counter them with some more realistic positive thinking. If not sleeping is a trigger for anxiety then the thought of "What am I going to do, I'm not going to sleep tonight", can be replaced by "Often I do sleep at night but if I'm not asleep after an hour in bed I can take a sleeping pill." This calms down the person and helps them to avoid anxiety. It's sounds easy, but to be effective a person has to spend time considering lots of different situations, writing down their responses and learning the ways that they can change their thinking.

Your therapist can tell you about Cognitive Behaviour Training and there are books available in most libraries. Many mental health care institutes offer this type of training in a group environment. The classes usually span over ten to twelve weeks. (See Appendix IV on Cognitive Behaviour Training.)

Positive thoughts

Whenever you are aware of negative thoughts, replace them with positive thoughts. Keep telling yourself you will be fine. Talk out loud to yourself and praise yourself for all the steps that you are taking to get well.

Meditation

Meditation is easy and inexpensive to start, just look for books and CDs in your local library. There are lots of forms of meditation but mostly they use calming music and a quiet voice to redirect your thoughts. One of the simplest methods is to concentrate on your breathing, just feel it flowing through the body. It sounds easy, but it does take practice to sustain an awareness of just the breathing to the exclusion of other thoughts. Meditation slows down the jumble of thoughts that crowd the mind and cause stress. As a result, you become calmer and less tired. It also gives your body time to heal.

Gupta's Amygdala Re-training

This treatment is for chronic fatigue but it was very effective for me against anxiety. I still use it if I feel flutters of that anxiety. It is similar to Cognitive Behaviour Training, but is based on talking out loud to yourself in a very positive way whenever you have anxious thoughts. The programme comes with a set of DVDs and a workbook and takes many months to complete. If you are interested in this, just google 'Gupta programme for chronic fatigue'. You'll know if you are in the right web site if it talks about amygdala re-training by Ashok Gupta.

Trust

And finally trust yourself, if you feel any particular therapy isn't working for you, you are probably right. Remember that anxious people were often schooled to discount their intuitive feelings and are very vulnerable in this world.

My journey took about ten years, but perhaps it could have taken a lot less if I had been more aware of the tools available to me. If you have anxiety, I hope this book will make you more aware of the help available. It is not a journey for the faint of heart, but often there is no alternative.

And if you have anxiety, you are not alone. Anxiety disorders are one of the most prevalent mental disorders in the world. One in thirteen people worldwide are thought to suffer from this condition and about three million people in Canada are estimated to suffer from anxiety. The best thing you can do for yourself is to see your doctor and seek help. Treatments are continually improving.

Appendix II

What is anxiety?

True anxiety is debilitating, all-consuming and relentless. Anyone who has suffered from this anxiety knows how overwhelming it is. It can last for days or more, with the person believing that it will never go away. And it can be so easily triggered. The thought that these destructive emotions can quickly appear again is, in itself, enough to cause more anxiety. It's exhausting and difficult to ignore. And then, it is difficult to find anything that will help when in immediate distress. No wonder an anxious person is spinning, trying to find something that will offer relief. If you've suffered from this anxiety, you can probably add your own descriptions.

But try explaining how you feel to those who don't suffer it. They just don't understand the overall intensity of the emotion. It is not like the mild anxiety that most people have experienced, perhaps before a job interview or a trip, or some other equally important event. That kind of mild anxiety is fleeting and ends once the event is past. It's just the body's mechanism of coping with a difficult situation.

In an anxiety disorder, the anxiety doesn't abate, the person continues to feel anxious just coping with their everyday life. They are stuck with thoughts that keep them in the anxiety and they are unable to see a way out of the feeling. They are out of control and just don't seem to be able to get back to a normal balance. They constantly feel threatened by things that might happen. It is illogical but unstoppable because the threat is mostly not real, but within the person's mind. Even if the anxiety feels as if it's about performance at work, relationship with people, fear of disease, fear of not sleeping, fear of flying, fear that something awful will happen, (the list is endless) it is more likely to be about basic insecurities. These insecurities may be caused by past experience or by genetics, both of which can make a person overly sensitive and unable to turn on self-soothing thoughts. If anxiety is becoming an uncontrollable part of your life, then it's time to seek help.

Appendix III

More about antidepressants

Antidepressants are the best medication available for controlling anxiety. That doesn't mean that a person with anxiety should take them. This is a very personal decision. Here is some information about them that may help you decide if they are right for you.

There are many different antidepressants available, each with their own range of conditions for which they are useful. So it's important to tell your doctor about all your symptoms then he/she can choose the best one for you.

Usually, your doctor will start you on a low dose to minimize any side effects which can include dry mouth, headache, nausea, dizziness or fatigue depending on the antidepressant. The more recently developed antidepressants have very little in the way of side effects. I only ever got a dry mouth and fatigue when I started on these medications. These side effects will go away after about two weeks as your body adjusts. Often, your doctor will ask to see you again in two weeks to check on your reaction to the medication. Then the doctor can decide if you need to change the medication or if you need a higher dose. Be aware that some antidepressants are not effective in some people. Your doctor may change your medication if it does not appear to have any benefits for you. The antidepressants that were effective for me were first Celexa, and then Effexor, but these medications are not effective for everybody's anxiety.

After a month of taking the medication, you should feel calmer and more upbeat about your life. Antidepressants are often referred to as 'happy pills' because they improve your mood and emotions. They were thought to work by balancing neurotransmitters, such as serotonin, in your brain, but this idea is not fully supported by recent scientific research. As it stands now, we do not clearly understand how they work, but we know they can be very effective for some people in controlling anxiety and depression. They do not change your underlying personality. You are still you. These medications are not addictive in the sense that you will continually need a higher dose for them to be effective. Your body, however, may become dependent on them to balance your moods. This is why it is so important never to stop them suddenly. In the longer term, the use of antidepressants may affect sexual function.

So how long can you expect to be taking the antidepressants? That depends on many factors. If you are doing emotional work to change your thinking patterns and changing your environment then your brain becomes healthier and more able to take back its role of balancing the neurotransmitters. This is especially true for those who suffer from depression. So maybe in a year or so you can consider stopping the medication but be careful—the dose needs to be lowered very slowly over a period of time so that your body can adjust. Your doctor will help you with this. For me, I've accepted that I'll probably be taking the medication for the rest of my life.

Of course, there's all kind of information on the World Wide Web about antidepressants, but you can fall down a never-ending rabbit hole researching this information. Go to respected sites, like the Mayo clinic or Medlineplus, a government site, which will give you lots of reliable information so that you can have questions for your doctor.

Finally, patience is needed with antidepressants, the desired cure does not come about immediately. Sometimes it may take months to find the right dose of the right antidepressant for you.

Appendix IV

Cognitive Behaviour Training

Anxiety is caused by the thought patterns of an individual. It can trap them in a vicious cycle of negative thoughts. Cognitive Behaviour Training (CBT) is a method of changing these thoughts to be more realistic, so the person no longer feels anxiety.

The first step is to identify situations that cause anxiety and then explore the kinds of thoughts that are associated with this. Many of these thoughts come up automatically, such as, "I always do the wrong thing." Often these thoughts are not based on facts.

The second step is to identify these negative thoughts so you can recognize your patterns of negative thinking. Then you look for real evidence to see if the negative thoughts are true. Often they are not.

The third step is to reshape your negative thoughts or inaccurate thinking with something more realistic and positive, such as, "Often I do the right thing, it's only occasionally that I make mistakes." But it can be difficult to come up with positive thoughts that you can truly accept. So the method takes lots of practice. Many different situations are considered and the person is encouraged to write each step down. In this way the person can see, that often, they do not think in a reasonable way and they over-dramatize the negative.

When this kind of training goes along with the emotional work of acknowledging one's past or present, it can be very powerful. There is strong evidence that these two together (CBT plus the emotional work) can be as good as antidepressants. All this sounds very promising but it is difficult to do on your own. There is an excellent workbook, *Mind over Mood – Change How You Feel and How You Think* by Greenberger and Padesky (check your library). This workbook takes you step by step though Cognitive Behaviour Training, it gives lots of examples and provides exercises where you can practice the skills. I was delighted by this book but I still felt I needed help using it. Also, by the time I discovered it, I was so deep into anxiety that exercises designed to help often put me into more anxiety.

Now I do use CBT on my sleeping. When I have the thought, *I'm not going to sleep tonight. What am I going to do?* I replace it with, *Usually I do sleep at night but if I don't sleep, I'll just be a little tired tomorrow.* This stops me from going into anxiety.

Even better than the workbook is to take a course on Cognitive Behaviour Training or discuss it with your therapist. Then you can get feedback on how to use it most effectively for you. But remember this process will be more effective if goes along with, or is used just after, any emotional work. You will also find useful information on this at the Mayo clinic web site.

Appendix V

Behavioural patterns common to many anxiety-prone people

Being in control

Most people who suffer from anxiety relieve it by avoiding situations that trigger it and controlling circumstances. If they're frightened of flying, they don't fly. If they're planning a trip and don't feel comfortable leaving home, they either don't go or they plan their trip right down to the last detail so nothing can go wrong. If things don't go as expected they tend to go into anxiety. Anxious people don't feel confident that they can deal with new situations. Of course, in reality, no-one can have complete control, unforeseen things are always going to happen. Trying to control everything puts a tremendous stress on a person and is such a waste of energy.

Trust

Anxious people often have a problem with trust. Usually anxious people are that way because they have been let down in some way in the past. Perhaps they were parented in a way that did not allow them to feel safe or maybe they have faced some catastrophic event in their lives. They are suspicious and wary of other people. They have difficulty delegating tasks to others, whether it's at home or work. Consequently, they tend to keep people at a distance from themselves. They build a wall and don't let others know how they are feeling or thinking. To say the least, this gets in the way of personal relationships. Anxious people are often lonely people. On the other hand, they can trust too easily, especially if they perceive that a person needs help. They can get very involved and then can be easily manipulated. All this happens because, often, they don't listen to their normal instincts.

Resistance to taking medication

Anxious people often resist taking medicine for their condition. Perhaps this has to do with the need to feel in control. The most commonly prescribed drugs for anxiety are antidepressants. They are mood-changers and help people to feel more positive about the world. But in the first two weeks of taking them, it's possible for the patient to experience uncomfortable side effects. These side effects are usually minor and go away as the body acclimatizes to the drugs. However, some anxious people feel that they are very sensitive to drugs and often experience many of the side effects causing them to stop treatment.

Lack of self confidence

Anxious people rarely feel confident in themselves. They feel that others and their opinions are more important than them. This leads to the behaviour of 'people pleasing' outlined in the next paragraph.

People pleasing and failure to draw boundaries

Anxious people tend to do things that they feel will please others. They also find it very difficult to say, 'No' if extra demands are asked of them. This is because they have a great deal of difficulty drawing boundaries. They don't recognize their own needs and don't make it clear to others when their boundaries are crossed.

They need to develop strategies of honouring themselves and speaking out when things are not right for them. Instead they erode their self esteem by putting them selves last.

Shoulds

Connected to the efforts to control everything, are all the 'shoulds' that seem to be embedded within anxious people. They feel they 'should' do this or that and feel guilty if they don't follow through.

Perfectionism

Anxious people feel they need to do things perfectly. This allows them to feel in control. Often they will spend a lot of time on small details that are not important. This attitude also makes decisions very difficult as they feel they must make the 'right' decision. Often, it doesn't occur to them that they can change their minds.

Obsessiveness

Associated with perfectionism and a desire to be in control is obsessive behaviour. Anxious people are often obsessive about many things, wanting to complete things and wanting to do things in the 'right' way.

Anger

Deep down anxious people are often very angry because they feel there is never any justice for them in this world.

Some consequences of these behaviours

The preceding behaviours can be very harmful. Trying to be in control, trying to be perfect and becoming angry alienate other people, cause resentment and result in loneliness for the person practising these behaviours. People pleasing and not trusting a person send out subtle vibes which cause others not to trust in return. Obsessiveness, "shoulds" and not drawing boundaries tie a person up in behaviours that may exhaust them. Lacking self-confidence often causes a person to feel ashamed about asking for help so they never get their needs met. They also anguish over decisions. It's all exhausting. It is so worthwhile, to recognize those behaviours which tie you down and then to get help in changing them.

Appendix VI

Chronic Fatigue Syndrome

Chronic Fatigue Syndrome is a complex condition that is not universally accepted in the medical community. There is debate as to whether this condition is a psychological disorder or a physical disorder. It is diagnosed when there is extreme fatigue that lasts for over six months and seems to have no underlying medical cause. The fatigue is not alleviated by normal rest and is exacerbated by any kind of physical activity. Some of the common symptoms are enlarged lymph nodes, dizziness when the person stands, muscle aches and pains, difficulty concentrating and bowel symptoms such as diarrhea. Many people develop Chronic Fatigue after a viral infection.

Long term anxiety can also lead to Chronic Fatigue because it overuses the hormones of Fight or Flight, adrenaline and cortisol. Anxiety, also exhausts the body and prevents self-soothing brain hormones from being released.

There is no standard treatment for Chronic Fatigue and there are very few Chronic Fatigue specialists available. Generally, rest and psychotherapy are the common treatments used.

Gupta's Amygdala retraining is available on the internet. The premise behind this treatment is that when there are deeply ingrained thought patterns revolving around fear, the amygdala is put on high alert. This is a primitive part of the brain that deals with fear. The result is that the amygdala causes the body to over react to external and internal stimuli. This causes all the aches and pains and exhausts the body.

The solution is to interrupt all the negative thoughts of anxiety with a verbal positive mantra. This is supposed to retrain the amygdala so that it no longer perceives overwhelming fear in the thoughts. With the removal of the fear stimulus, the amygdala will calm down and stop causing the body to over react.

In some ways the Gupta's Amygdala Retraining is like Cognitive Behaviour Training, but the physical component of talking out loud seems to increase its effectiveness.

Appendix VII

Genetics and anxiety

Why do some people develop mental problems and others do not? Part of this may be due to genetics. Certainly mental illness can be traced through families. If certain genes for the functioning of the brain or for chemicals in the brain are faulty, then a person may have a predisposition to mental disorders. But certainly, environment plays a role as well. There is much evidence to show that if a person experiences trauma, they are more at risk of developing mental problems.

Biological research has also come up with some interesting discoveries concerning our genetic make-up. Genes do control our character, to a degree, and with certain environmental conditions, genes can be turned on or off. This is the relatively new study of epigenetics. It shows that there is an echo of anxiety that reverberates from one generation to the next, depending on which genes get turned on and off in an individual by the environment.

There is an interesting piece of research on mammals by Michael Meaney and Moshe Szyf. They found that if a parent rat licked her young frequently then those individual babies grew up to be calm, less-stressed adults. However if the young were not licked regularly they became stressed as adults. But, most importantly, there were changes to a portion of the DNA. It became tightly wound up and the genes on this portion could not work. This research carried out in 2004 was the first evidence of maternal behaviour having an impact on the expression of the offspring's genes. We all have, in our genetic makeup, self-soothing genes but, according to this research, childhood conditions or a traumatic shock can turn these genes off, then we can become worried and feel unsafe in the world, more easily. It is thought that this is what happens with post-traumatic stress. Certain genes are turned off and the body no longer has the ability to soothe itself. The treatment for this is to find ways of soothing one's self. There is evidence that genes that have been turned off can be turned back on again. Perhaps, antidepressants and Cognitive Behaviour Training increase the body's ability to soothe itself by turning self-soothing genes back on. Epigenetics is an exciting new area of research that will not only have an impact on mental illnesses, but also on many other diseases.